THE DIVINE DRAMA®

OUR NARRATIVE

Fourth Edition

Harry Wendt

CROSSWAYS INTERNATIONAL
Minneapolis, MN

THE DIVINE DRAMA®—Our Narrative
was developed and written by
Harry Wendt, Minneapolis, MN

Illustrations by
Knarelle Beard, Adelaide, South Australia

The Bible text in this publication is from the New Revised Standard Version of the Bible,
copyright 1989 by the Division of Christian Education of the National Council of
Churches of Christ in the United States of America and used by permission.

THE DIVINE DRAMA®—Our Narrative
is published and distributed by
CROSSWAYS INTERNATIONAL
7930 Computer Avenue South
Minneapolis, MN 55435

ISBN 1-891245-10-4

Fourth Edition
10 9 8 7 6 5

Foreword

Early in 1993, it was my privilege to meet Dr. Andrew Hsaio, the President of the Lutheran Theological Seminary in Hong Kong. Dr. Hsaio was forced to leave China in 1948, and for 31 years was not permitted to return to visit his relatives.

In 1979, Dr. Hsaio and his wife were finally able to travel by train from Hong Kong to his home town in Hunan Province. His relatives, whom he had not seen since leaving China, were waiting on the platform to greet him. One of the group approached him, and asked, "Andrew, do you know who I am?" Dr. Hsaio looked at him for a moment or two, and replied, "I am sorry. I do not recognize you." The man replied, "Andrew, I am your brother-in-law." And what was the next question the brother-in-law asked? It was, "Andrew, did you bring us some Bibles?" To which Dr. Hsaio replied, "I brought you ten!" His brother-in-law responded, "Praise God!"

Dr. Hsaio tells of a pastor in China who had prayed for years that God would help him get a Bible. One day this pastor met a tourist who kindly gave him his Bible. He rushed home to his wife, and told her the good news! His prayers had been answered! He now had a Bible! She responded, "Why didn't you pray for two Bibles? I want one too!" He thought for while, and then answered, "I will get you one!" So, during the year that followed, he made a copy of his Bible by hand—and gave it to his wife!

In the affluent Western world, there is no shortage of Bibles. However, there is a shortage of people prepared to devote life to reading it with passion. And we are paying a price for our neglect!

If people are to make sense out of the Bible, three things are important:

 We need to know the biblical story-line (*narrative analysis*). (It is important, therefore, that you work through **See Through the Scriptures**, **THE DIVINE DRAMA—The Biblical Narrative**, or **Crossways** prior to studying this manual.)

 We need to know something about the themes that weave their way through the story-line (*narrative theology*).

 We need to see what Jesus does with the biblical story-line and its themes (*systematize Jesus' teachings*).

This study manual is offered to the people of God around the world in the hope that it will persuade more to become "biblical bloodhounds" whose one desire in life is to make *spiritual sense* out of the *biblical scents!*

Dr. Harry Wendt
Minneapolis, MN

Note: At the end of each unit is a section titled *POINTS TO PONDER*. It sums up the main points in each unit. The points summarize the central message of the illustrations in each unit.

Contents

THE DIVINE DRAMA®

OUR NARRATIVE

UNIT 17
Some Biblical Basics

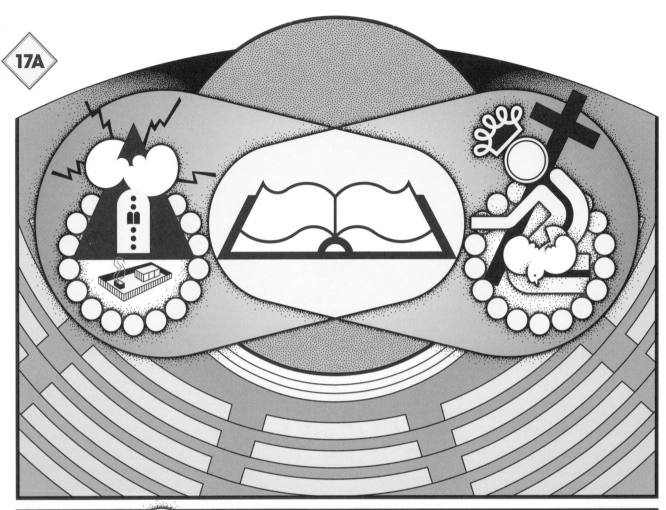

TODAY

Upper section

 As we work our way through the **Bible**, we sense that it is the script for a huge drama. Although the stage (**blue, circular stage**) for that drama is Planet Earth—in particular that region we today refer to as the Middle East—we become increasingly aware that we are not merely spectators of the drama watching events from a distance (**seats in amphitheater**). We are all on stage—and participating!

 Two major events emerge within the biblical narrative. The *first* has to do with God rescuing the Israelites from slavery in Egypt and making a covenant with them at Sinai (*Exodus 1*). The *second* has to do with the mission and ministry of Jesus the Messiah (*Exodus 2*).

 Upper left

When God gathered the Israelites in *community* (**circle of small circles**) around *Mt. Sinai* (**triangular-shaped mountain**), God's divine presence at the top of the mountain took the form of a **storm cloud** and **lightning**. God then made a covenant with the people (**symbol for covenant, with five dots and law-tablets**). The book of Exodus also speaks of God taking up residence among the Israelites in the **Tabernacle** they built at Sinai.

 Upper right

The New Testament describes how God entered into history clothed in flesh in the person of Jesus the Messiah. Jesus, the **Servant-King**, lived a sinless life—a life that was a display of God's Kingdom in action. Jesus permitted humanity to crucify Him (**cross**) so that He might win for them the forgiveness of sin, and rescue them from death and eternal judgment. The Holy Spirit (**dove**) continues to make known Jesus' saving mission and ministry, and to inspire and empower those who believe in Jesus to live in servant community (**circle of small circles**) and to reflect His mind and manner.

Lower section

The segments of the winding path refer to blocks of events within the sweep of biblical history.

- ◆ **Cloud:** God created the universe, Genesis chs.1,2. God's presence is depicted by a cloud several times in the biblical narrative, Exodus 19:16-18; 1 Kings 8:10,11; Luke 9:34; Acts 1:9.

- ◆ **First black section:** God was involved in all of the history of humanity prior to the call of Abraham, Genesis 1–11.

- ◆ **First orange section:** God was involved in the history of humanity and the Israelites throughout the period described in the Old Testament.

- ◆ **Second black section:** Jewish writings produced "between the Testaments" (namely, the *Apocrypha* and *Pseudepigrapha*) reveal events and beliefs relating to the history of the Jewish people during that period.

- ◆ **Second orange section:** The New Testament presents God's **final truth** as revealed in Jesus the Messiah's **servant life**, **crucifixion**, **burial**, **resurrection**, and **ascension**.

- ◆ **Dove, third black section:** Since Jesus' ascension, the Holy Spirit has continued to make known the meaning of Jesus' mission and ministry for humanity, and will continue to do so until Jesus reappears at the end of time.

In the upper segment of **ILLUSTRATION 17B** are the *symbol for God*, a *cloud* symbolizing God's presence, and God's *written Word*, the **Bible**. The *spirals* protruding from the Bible point to God at work within creation and the sweep of history.

 First spiral: Genesis 1:1-2:25 refers to God "speaking" His Word of power to bring creation into existence, and to set human history in motion.

 Second spiral: The major event described in the Old Testament has to do with God rescuing the Israelites from Egypt, gathering them (*people holding hands in community*) around His presence (*cloud*, *lightning*) at **Mt. Sinai**, and making a *covenant* with them. The prophets (*person within symbol for covenant*) based their ministry and proclamations on the contents and spirit of the Sinai covenant.

 Third and fourth spirals: As the history of God's people unfolded, some prophets drew on what earlier prophets had said, and applied it to a *later* situation. All prophets pointed the people to the same truths—to God's past and present actions on behalf of His people, and God's will for their lives.

 Fifth spiral: The New Testament reveals that the God who created the universe, the God who involved Himself in the history of ancient Israel, *finally became a flesh-and-blood person* in Jesus the Servant-Messiah:

- ◆ the Messianic King (*Servant-King*),
- ◆ who was crucified (*cross*)
- ◆ and buried (*tomb*),
- ◆ has risen from the dead (*open tomb*), and,
- ◆ beyond His ascension (*rising arrow*)
- ◆ fills the universe (*cloud*, *symbol for the divine presence*).

Beyond Jesus' ascension, the Holy Spirit (*dove*) continues to make known Jesus' saving mission.

 Sixth spiral: The New Testament reveals that the Lord who created the universe and humanity will eventually bring history and time to an end, gather all people before Him for what the Scriptures refer to as the "final judgment" (Matthew 25:31-46), and usher in eternity—that age which will have no end.

The prophets often proclaimed *words of doom* for the present, and *words of hope* for the future. However, they did not always understand how their words would come to final fulfillment. We might compare their preaching to people today who drive towards a mountain range. They see high peaks ahead, and drive up them. When they reach what they thought was the summit, they see an even higher line of peaks, and eventually another, and continue until they reach the highest point—one which they could not have seen from the plain below (*red dashed lines*).

Although the prophets might not always have understood or seen how their God-given message would finally be fulfilled, God is not limited by human horizons. God is above and beyond all human "mountain peaks." God knew what His Word would accomplish at the time when a prophet spoke, and what it would again accomplish in the centuries beyond. God's ultimate Word broke into creation and history in Jesus the Messiah, Hebrews 1:1-3. **Jesus, as God's Word in human flesh and form, is the final interpretation and interpreter of all Old Testament writings and events.**

The Word Made Flesh

ILLUSTRATION 17C depicts in graphic form Martin Luther's statement, "The Bible is the cradle that brings us Jesus of Nazareth." New Testament writings support and amplify this insight.

The Word in Judaism

 The rabbis, or Jewish teachers, of Jesus' day taught that the first thing God created was the *Torah*, the Pentateuch, the first five books of Moses. They said that although the Torah was created before the universe, God eventually *dictated* it to Moses at Sinai. They also said that although other books in the Jewish scriptures were *inspired by God*, God did not *dictate* their contents word by word.

 Some rabbis equated the Torah with *Wisdom*, and said that Wisdom was not only the blueprint on which creation was based, but the very architect of creation; see Proverbs 8:23, 27. In other words, they thought of Wisdom as a person. Some identified Wisdom with the written Law, and insisted that Wisdom dwelt only in Israel, Sirach 24:3,4. (Sirach is a Jewish Apocryphal book. Although it is not part of the Hebrew Scriptures, some Christian groups include it and other Apocryphal books in their Bible.)

 Rabbis referred to the Torah as *the bread of life*, *the water of life*, and *the light of the world*.

The Word in the New Testament

 The New Testament teaches that, in Jesus, the Word of God became a Person, John 1:14. God's "final word" to humanity is seen and heard in Jesus, Hebrews 1:1-4.

 Matthew teaches that in Jesus:

- ◆ One greater than the *Temple* has come, 12:6.
- ◆ One greater than the *Sabbath* has come, 12:8. (The observance of the Sabbath receives much attention in Exodus 20:8-11 and Deuteronomy 5:12-15.)
- ◆ One greater than *Jonah* has come, 12:41. (Jonah was sent to preach to the Gentiles.)
- ◆ One greater than *Solomon* has come, 12:42. (Compare Matthew 2:11 with 1 Kings 10:23-25. Note 1 Corinthians 1:24.)

These pronouncements would have greatly angered Jesus' hearers.

 John speaks of Jesus as:

- ◆ *The bread of life*, 6:41
- ◆ *The water of life*, 4:7-15
- ◆ *The light of the world*, 8:12, 9:5.

The *written Word* points beyond itself to the *Living Word, Jesus the Messiah*.

Jesus, the Pivotal Point

 The life and ministry of Jesus the Messiah forms the *grand finale* of **THE DIVINE DRAMA—The Biblical Narrative**. Jesus will remain central throughout **THE DIVINE DRAMA—Our Narrative**.

ILLUSTRATION 17D summarizes key events and truths in relation to Jesus the Messiah.

    a.   ***Servant-King:*** Jesus' servant life.

    b.   ***Cross:*** Jesus' crucifixion.

    c.   ***Tomb:*** Jesus' burial.

    d.   ***Open tomb:*** Jesus' resurrection.

    e.   ***Rising arrow:*** Jesus' ascension. Later units will point out that when Jesus "ascended," Jesus did not withdraw His presence, but transformed it. Jesus remains among us, although invisibly. We live out life before Jesus' eyes.

    f.   ***Glorified Jesus at God's right hand:*** The Father, who vindicated Jesus in the resurrection (that is, gave Jesus a "yes—I approve!" vote by raising Him from the dead), has given Him authority over the universe. Jesus the Messiah is Lord of creation, time, and eternity.

 The units that follow will focus on how God draws people into a relationship with Jesus.

    a.   ***Bible:*** The Bible points to Jesus as the key to its message, John 5:39.

    b.   ***Drop of water:*** Through baptism, God adopts people into Jesus' family, and makes them partakers of and sharers in all that Jesus accomplished, Galatians 4:3–7; Romans 6:1-23.

    c.   ***Bread and cup:*** In Holy Communion, Christians dine at Jesus' table, Luke 24:30,31. They celebrate what they are, and go forth to become what they eat.

 When God brings people to faith in Jesus the Messiah, God gathers them into His family, His community (people holding hands in community). In that community, they thank and praise God for what God has done for them through Jesus the Messiah (***figure with hands raised***, *lower left*), and serve Jesus by serving others (***servant figure***, *lower right*).

 The goal of **THE DIVINE DRAMA—Our Narrative**, is to help you make the following hymn verse your personal prayer:

> *O let me see Your footmarks*
> > *And in them plant my own;*
> *My hope to follow duly*
> > *Is in Your strength alone.*
> *O guide me, call me, draw me,*
> > *Uphold me to the end;*
> *And then in heaven receive me,*
> > *My Savior and my friend.*

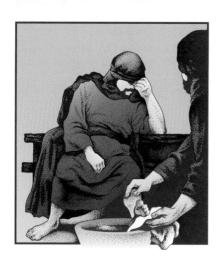

17A **The goal of God's divine drama is to restore all people to eternal fellowship with God and one another through Jesus the Messiah.** The *key word* throughout the Bible is *grace* (*undeserved mercy and goodness*). The *means* God uses to establish a relationship with people is *the forgiveness of sins*. God achieved His plan through the life, death, and resurrection of Jesus the Messiah.

17B Christians speak of the Bible as God's inspired, written Word. At the same time, the *written Word* (*Bible*) points beyond itself to God's *Living Word* (*Jesus*) at work in creation and history.

◆ God's Word created the universe, and now sustains it.

◆ God's Word, spoken through the prophets, directed Israel's history and disciplined the nation.

◆ **God's creative and prophetic Word finally became a person in Jesus of Nazareth.** In Jesus, God's plan for creation and history became visible. Jesus was and is God's Word in flesh-and-blood form. We can see and read God's Word in Jesus' life and ministry. Jesus, God's final Word, declares humanity forgiven, gathers people into God's Kingdom, and calls them to live as servants of God and others, just as Jesus was the perfect Servant.

17C Although it is most important that God's people (and humanity at large!) read the written Scriptures carefully and zealously, the true and final Word of God is Jesus Himself. Throughout His ministry, the visible Jesus revealed—through His words and actions— the heart, mind, and will of His invisible Father.

17D There is no such thing as *private* Christianity. Christianity is always a *community* affair. Through *Baptism*, God adopts us into Jesus' family. In *Holy Communion* (*The Lord's Supper*, *Eucharist*), Jesus invites us to dine with Him, and gives Himself to us through bread and wine. Those who belong to Jesus' family are to thank and praise God for all He has done, still does, and will do. They are also to serve one another in a way that reflects the mind and manner of Jesus.

THE DIVINE DRAMA®

OUR NARRATIVE

UNIT 18
Our Baptismal Exodus

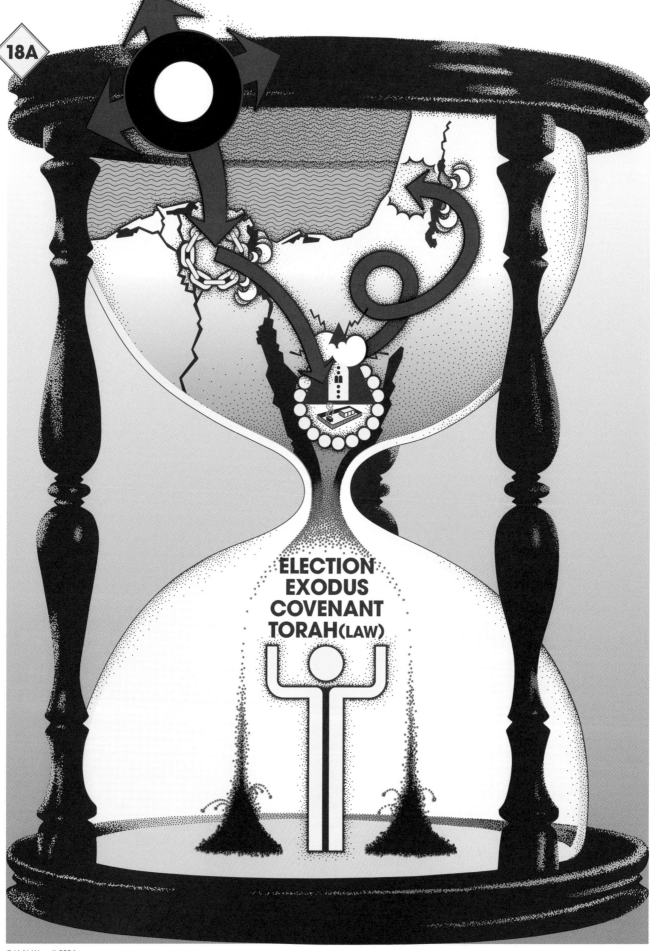

ELECTION
EXODUS
COVENANT
TORAH(LAW)

 In 1620, the Pilgrim colonists came to the United States on the *Mayflower*. In 1770, Captain James Cook, on the *Endeavor*, explored the east coast of Australia and claimed it for England. Was anybody who is living today on board the *Mayflower* or the *Endeavor*? We say, "No! Life began for us only during the past century. We did not take part in events that took place hundreds of years ago." When people who live in the Western world think about past events, they remember them in the sense of *recalling* them.

 When the ancient Israelites thought about and celebrated past events, they saw themselves as *re-membered* to—joined to, linked to, and participating as *members* in—those events. For example, when they offered their first fruits to God, they were to confess the following creed:

> *You shall make this response before the Lord your God, "A wandering Aramean [Jacob] was my ancestor; <u>he</u> went down into Egypt and lived there as an alien, few in number; and there <u>he</u> became a great nation, mighty and populous. When the Egyptians treated <u>us</u> harshly and afflicted <u>us</u>, by imposing hard labor on <u>us</u>, <u>we</u> cried to the LORD, the God of our ancestors; the LORD heard <u>our</u> voice and saw <u>our</u> affliction, <u>our</u> toil, and <u>our</u> oppression. The LORD brought <u>us</u> out of Egypt with a mighty hand and an outstretched arm, with a terrifying display of power, and with signs and wonders; and he brought <u>us</u> into this place and gave <u>us</u> this land, a land flowing with milk and honey.* (Deuteronomy 26:5–9)

The words underlined above emphasize the change that takes place in the creed from *third* to *first* person. The <u>he</u> becomes <u>we</u>, <u>us</u>, and <u>our</u>. The passage illustrates vividly how the ancient Israelites remembered the past.

 ILLUSTRATION 18A makes use of an **hourglass** to depict how the ancient Israelites understood themselves as being "membered to" past events, in that they saw the sands of past events (**the Exodus from Egypt**, *upper section*) flowing around their *present history* (**person**, *lower section*). Throughout their history, the Jewish people have celebrated their belief that they are God's "chosen people" (**ELECTION**), that God rescued them from Egypt in the **EXODUS** event, that God made a **COVENANT** with them at Sinai, and that God gave them the **TORAH (LAW)**—Genesis, Exodus, Leviticus, Numbers, Deuteronomy—at Sinai. The Old Testament commands Jews to "re-member" this way, Deuteronomy 6:20–25, Joshua 4:19–24. Still today, they celebrate their participation in these events.

18B

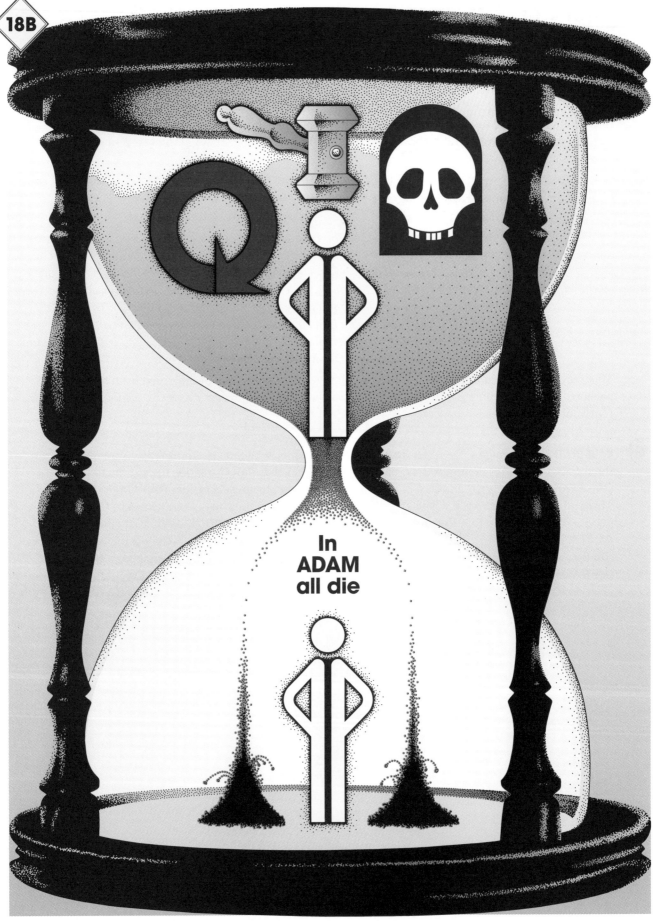

In
ADAM
all die

Already before Jesus began His public ministry, John the Baptist called the Jewish people to repentance, and warned them that the fact that they were descendants of Abraham did not contribute to their status before God, Matthew 3:7-10.

After Jesus' ascension, His disciples (now apostles, meaning "those sent" to proclaim what they learned as disciples) and followers began witnessing to their Jewish brothers and sisters. Many of the people to whom they witnessed insisted that they did not need a savior. They had the Law that God gave to Moses at Mt. Sinai. Some thought they were special because of their Jewish genes. They were descendants of Abraham. They looked on themselves as God's chosen people.

Paul answered them: "You have not gone back far enough! You are misguided in merely going back to Abraham, and taking pride in your physical descent from Him. You must go back beyond Abraham to Adam and give thought to your link to him. We are all descendants of Adam and we all share Adam's fall into sin, and its consequences. In Adam, we all die!" Paul deals with the implications of humanity's link to, and descent from, Adam in the following verses in Romans 5.

- ◆ "Therefore, just as sin came into the world through one man (i.e. *Adam*) and death through sin, and so death spread to all because all have sinned," 5:12.
- ◆ "For if many died through the one man's trespass," 5:15b.
- ◆ "For the judgment following one trespass brought condemnation," 5:16b.
- ◆ "If, because of the one man's trespass, death exercised dominion through that one," 5:17.
- ◆ "Therefore, just as one man's trespass led to condemnation for all," 5:18.
- ◆ "For just as by the one man's disobedience the many were made sinners," 5:19.

Although the ancient Israelites could say, "The history of the fathers is my history. I was there!" Paul reminds them, *"Adam's history is our history. The human race, including us, took part in the fall into sin in Eden."*

In **ILLUSTRATION 18B**, the details in the *upper section* of the **hourglass** depict *Adam* (**yellow figure**), his *rebellion* (**symbol for sin**), and the resulting *judgment* (**gavel**), *death* and *condemnation* (**tombstone with skull**). Adam's fall flows into and influences the present. *Humanity* (**person**, *lower section*) shares its consequences—**In ADAM all die**. *The sands of time from Adam flow around humanity today.*

Paul's awareness of sharing in Adam's plight caused him to cry out, "Wretched man that I am! Who will rescue me from this body of death?" Romans 7:24. **ILLUSTRATION 18C** will depict Paul's answer.

BECOME
what you are

The spiritual song asks, "Were you there when they crucified my Lord?" It expects the answer, "Yes, I was there! I saw it happen!" The New Testament assures baptized Christians that they did not merely *watch* the crucifixion. They *shared* it. They *experienced* it. Paul writes:

> For surely you know that when we were baptized into union with Christ Jesus, we were baptized into union with His death. By our baptism, then, we were buried with Him and shared His death, in order that just as Christ was raised from death by the glorious power of the Father, so also we might live a new life. (Romans 6:3,4, TEV translation; see also Romans 6:5–8)

By virtue of our physical birth, we share in *Adam* (**ILLUSTRATION 18B**). By virtue of our second birth in baptism, we share in *Christ Jesus*, in *Jesus the Messiah*.

ILLUSTRATION 18C depicts Jesus' saving actions for us (*upper section*) and our sharing in them (*lower section*) through *baptism* (**drop of water**) and the *Holy Spirit* (**dove**) in the neck of the **hourglass**.

Upper section

 When Jesus led a sinless life (***Servant-King***), we, by virtue of our baptism, led it with Him. When Jesus was put to death to suffer the punishment for humanity's sin (***cross***), we, by virtue of our baptism, shared that death with Him. When Jesus was placed in the grave that sin brings (***tomb***), we, by virtue of our baptism, went into that grave with Him. When Jesus rose triumphant from the grave (***open tomb***, ***rising arrow***, ***glorified Jesus***), we, by virtue of our baptism, rose with Him, Ephesians 2:5,6.

 In Jesus the Messiah, God gathered the human race into one Person. God let that one Person be what God intended the human race to be, and to suffer what the human race deserves to suffer. In our baptism, God makes us participants in all that Jesus lived, suffered, endured, and conquered. God incorporates us into Jesus' saving ministry and mission.

Lower section

 In Jesus, God has declared us to be holy, 1 Corinthians 1:1,2. God has given us Jesus' sinless life, death, and resurrection as a set of credentials to possess as our very own. When we stand before God on the last day of history, we shall show God Jesus' credentials—not our own. **On that Last Day of history, God will welcome us Home, not on the basis of what we have achieved, but on the basis of what Jesus has achieved for us.**

 While we wait for the Last Day, God's appeal is: "Seek to demonstrate in your own life the life you have been given. ***BECOME what you are!*** Live out what I have declared you to be!" To understand this is to grasp the wonder of our high calling in Jesus the Messiah.

In relation to the truths depicted in **ILLUSTRATION 18B** and **ILLUSTRATION 18C**, Paul writes:

> For since death came through a human being, the resurrection of the dead has also come through a human being; for as all die in Adam, so all will be made alive in Christ. (1 Corinthians 15:21,22)

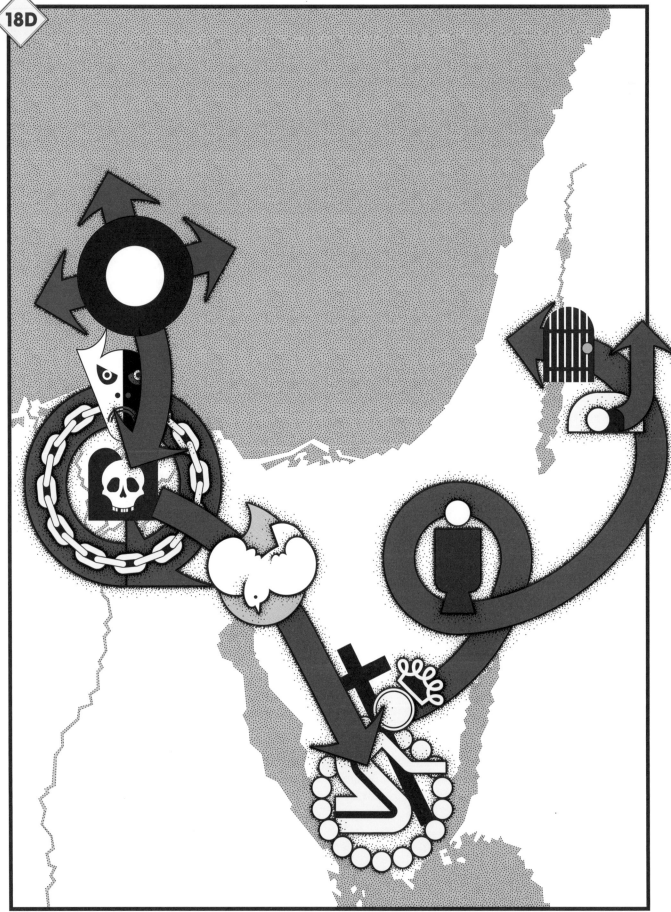

Our Baptismal Exodus Experience

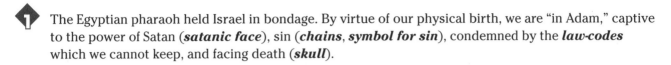

ILLUSTRATION 18D depicts the parallels between our baptism and the events of the Exodus from Egypt, the wilderness wanderings, and the entry into the Promised Land.

1 The Egyptian pharaoh held Israel in bondage. By virtue of our physical birth, we are "in Adam," captive to the power of Satan (**satanic face**), sin (**chains**, **symbol for sin**), condemned by the **law-codes** which we cannot keep, and facing death (**skull**).

2 God broke into Israel's bondage in Egypt and opened up a way for the people to pass through the waters. Similarly, the Holy Spirit (**dove**) works through Holy Baptism (**drop of wate**r) to lead us out of our bondage to Satan, sin, and death into fellowship with Jesus.

3 God gathered the community of ancient Israel around Himself at Sinai. Similarly, through Holy Baptism God gathers us into the community of Jesus (**circle of small circles around the Servant-King carrying His cross**).

4 God dwelt among the Israelites people and led them through the wilderness to the Promised Land. Similarly, Jesus dwells among His people and guides them on their way through the wilderness of this life to the Eternal Promised Land, 1 Peter 1:3–8.

5 As God fed the Israelites during their forty years in the wilderness, so God sustains and strengthens His people through a Holy Meal, the Lord's Supper (**bread and cup**).

6 God opened a path through the Jordan River to enable the Israelites people to enter the land long before promised to Abraham. Similarly, through His victory over death (**open tomb**, **rising arrow**), Jesus has opened up the way for us to pass through that *final Jordan* called "death" (**tombstone with skull**) into the Heavenly Promised Land—into that final "inheritance that is imperishable, undefiled, and unfading, kept in heaven for us," 1 Peter 1:4,5. In Jesus, we already possess the Eternal Promised Land; we merely wait to enter what we already possess.

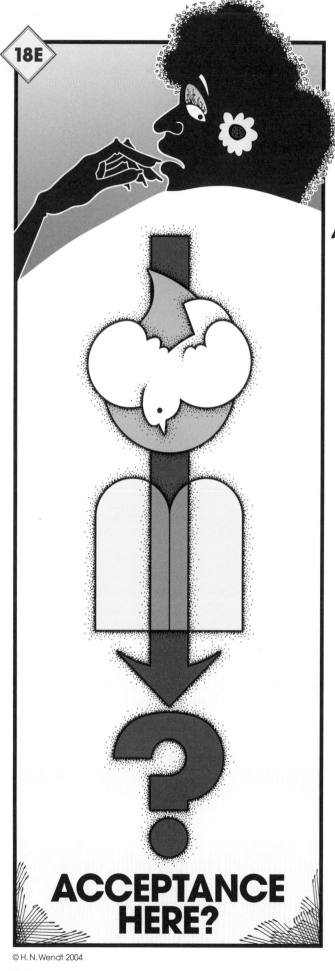

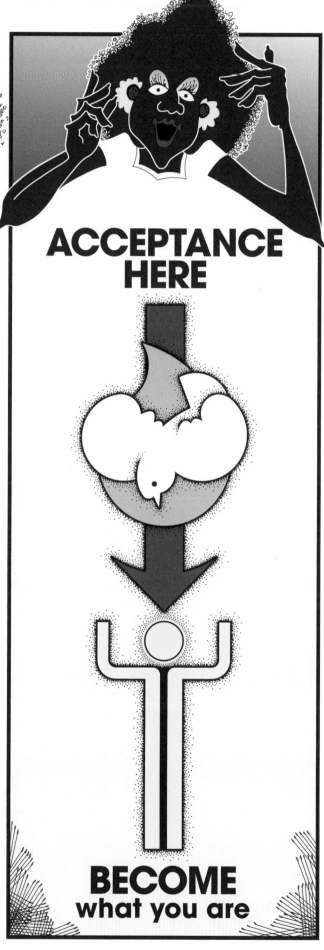

Left section

ACCEPTANCE HERE?

The person depicted appears doubtful. She thinks, "Yes, I was baptized, but how can I know if I have done enough good for God to accept me?" She is in doubt because she links her hope of salvation in part to her own achievements. She believes that through Holy Baptism (***drop of water***), the Holy Spirit (***dove***) gives her an opportunity to try to save herself by obedience to God's commandments (***law-codes***). Her thinking is incorrect.

Sadly and unfortunately, many people think that although God does 90% of what is necessary for salvation, we humans must also contribute something—even if it is only 10%. They do not understand the wonder of God's forgiving grace, and that Jesus did everything necessary to win salvation for us.

Right section

BECOME what you are

In describing our present status before God, the Bible says:

> *Beloved, we are God's children now.* (1 John 3:2)
>
> *There is therefore now no condemnation for those who are in Christ Jesus.* (Romans 8:1)
>
> *Who will bring any charge against God's elect? It is God who justifies.* (Romans 8:33)

The person depicted feels deep joy. She knows God loves her. She knows she is already God's child. God has already accepted her. God did this in her baptism when God shared with her what He achieved through the life, death, and resurrection of Jesus the Messiah. Her obedience is not an attempt to earn acceptance. It merely expresses her joy and gratitude to God for making her God's child—her desire to "become what she already is."

God's decision to accept us is based on God's forgiving, merciful kindness in Jesus the Messiah—nothing else. God is not influenced by:

◆ *The amount of water used in baptism,* or the manner in which we come into contact with it. God's word of promise, spoken together with the application of water, saves us. The water symbolizes what God's Word promises and achieves!

◆ *Our age when baptized.* God's power to save is not affected by our ability to understand the great things God does for us in Holy Baptism.

◆ *Anything we do during our baptism.* In Holy Baptism, God makes a decision for us, and commits Himself to us. Holy Baptism is a sacrament in which God adopts us. It is not a ceremony in which we commit ourselves to God, Titus 3:4–7; 1 Peter 3:21,22.

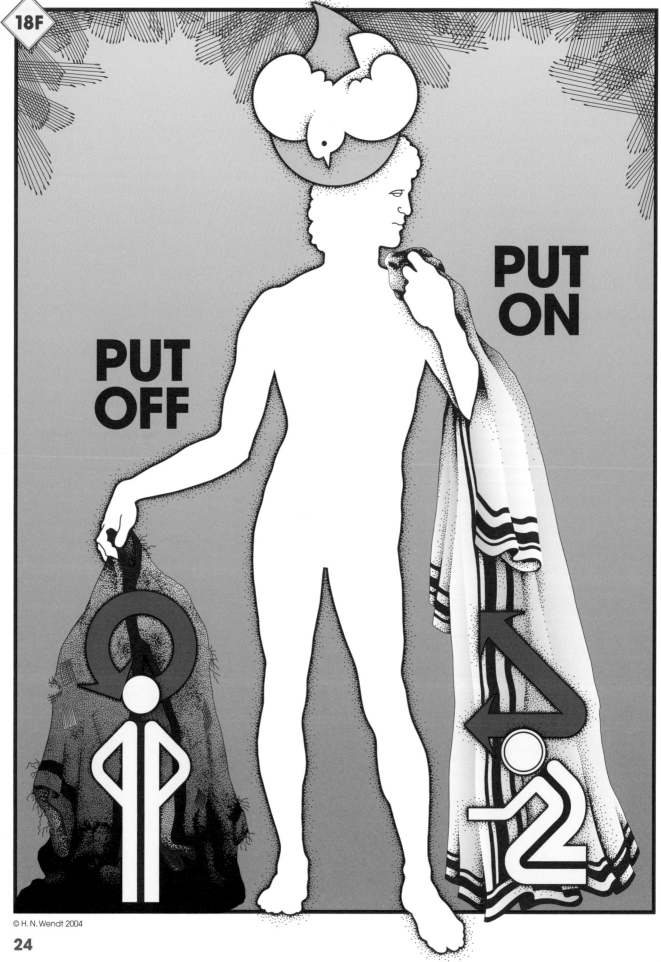

PUT
ON

PUT
OFF

 When the Holy Spirit (***dove***) gathers us into God's family through Holy Baptism (***drop of water***), our risen Lord, Jesus the Messiah, calls and empowers us to practice an ongoing undressing-dressing routine.

    a. Jesus summons us to "***PUT OFF***" our old way of life—of living for ourselves and letting our own inner whims, desires, and appetites control us (***dirty tattered garment***, ***person in posture of indifference***, ***symbol for sin***, *lower left*).

    b. Jesus summons us to "***PUT ON***" His way of life, to let Jesus inspire and empower us to speak, think, and act as He did (***clean garment***, ***Servant Jesus as our model***, *lower right*) in all we do as we walk through life in this world, Romans 8:9–11; Galatians 2:20.

 The *put-off/put-on* routine involves us in a struggle. By nature, we do not want to put off the old clothes, the old ways of life. We prefer them. We feel comfortable in them. Luther points out that we need to deal severely with the "old nature" and to "drown" it daily in the waters of our baptism. (Unfortunately, the old nature learns to tread water very well!)

 The daily struggle within us to *put-off* and *put-on* assures us that we are taking Jesus seriously, that our faith in Him is alive, and that our ongoing desire is not merely to embrace Jesus as our Savior but also to follow Him as our Lord. The Bible contains numerous put-off/put-on appeals.

> *You were taught to put away your former way of life, your old self, corrupt and deluded by its lusts, and to be renewed in the spirit of your minds, and to clothe yourselves with the new self, created according to the likeness of God in true righteousness and holiness.* (Ephesians 4:22–24)

> *Do not lie to one another, seeing that you have stripped off the old nature with its practices and have clothed yourselves with the new self which is being renewed in knowledge according to the image of its creator.* (Colossians 3:9,10)

18G

Copy Christ!

 Most schoolrooms around the world are equipped with a chalkboard or whiteboard. Often the alphabet is written in perfect script across the top of the board. Students are encouraged to improve their writing skills by studying it, copying it, comparing their efforts with it, and striving to improve their writing style.

 Peter wrote his first letter to Christians in Asia Minor (**one of these early Christians with arms raised in praise**, *lower center*). They were enduring difficulties. People within the community were ridiculing them because of their faith (**hostile face**, *lower left*). The threat of a Roman persecution hovered on the horizon (**Roman helmet and sword**, *lower right*). Peter wrote to give his readers encouragement and hope, and to help them deal with daily life. He pointed them to Jesus' life as the model for their own life:

> Christ also suffered for you, leaving you an example, so that you should follow in his steps. (1 Peter 2:21)

 Peter uses a vivid Greek term for "example." It refers to the perfect line of writing referred to in point 1 above. His appeal is: "Throughout your life, study Jesus' life. Remember that Jesus always did His Father's will, and served others as His Father wanted them to be served. Copy Jesus in everything you do!"

 Peter goes into detail about how we are to put his appeal into practice. He gives directions for living to: servants, 2:18; wives, 3:1; husbands, 3:7; to all Christians, 3:8,9.

Although during this earthly life we graduate from earthly schools, we dare never graduate from Jesus' "discipleship school."

The terms "repent" and "convert" are frequently used in Christian circles. What do they mean?

Upper section

Repentance

The word "repentance" literally means *to reconsider*, and refers to a profound change of mind, to a transformation of thinking patterns and value systems. The illustration depicts a person:

① *arrow:* who has *removed from her mind* all thought of living for self (***symbol for sin***), and

② *arrow:* whose constant desire is to fill her mind with the thoughts of God's forgiving love (***symbols for God***), and God's will for her life as revealed in her Savior and Lord, Jesus the Servant-Messiah (***Servant-King***).

Lower section

Convert

The word "convert" means literally "to turn around," as when a person walking in one direction stops, turns around, and walks in the opposite direction (***arrow depicting change in direction from sin to servanthood***).

In the Christian context, conversion refers to the total about-face that takes place in people's attitudes towards God and neighbor when they come to a knowledge of their sin and to faith in Jesus. Paul writes:

> *It is God who is at work in you, enabling you both to* will *and to* work *for his good pleasure.* (Philippians 2:13)

18A Biblical thinking about *remembering* is different from contemporary Western-world thinking. In biblical times, those who *remembered* past events thought of themselves as *having taken part* in those events. Hence, today Jews still speak of themselves as having taken part in the original Exodus-Sinai events.

18B Similarly, the New Testament suggests that the entire human race participated in Adam's first sin in Eden, and consequently still today shares Adam's guilt, judgment, and condemnation.

18C In Baptism, we are made participants in Jesus' saving work: His perfect servant life, death, burial, resurrection, and eternal life. Having been given Jesus' perfect Servant life, Christians are to demonstrate what they have been given.

18D The New Testament bases its presentation of God's plan of salvation on the Old Testament Exodus-Sinai series of events, but reinterprets them around Jesus' mission and ministry.

18E In Baptism, God does not merely give us an *opportunity* to persuade Him to accept us; God actually *accepts us* and *adopts us* into His family.

18F As God's adopted children, baptized Christians are to strive daily to *put off* their old, selfish ways of living, and to *put on* Jesus' new way of life.

18G The Christian's model for life is Jesus' life. We are to study Jesus' life constantly, and seek the Holy Spirit's guidance and power to conform our lives to Jesus' life.

18H Day by day, we are to pray to God for help *to think* Jesus' thoughts and *to live* Jesus' way.

THE DIVINE DRAMA®

OUR NARRATIVE

UNIT 19

**Blessed Be the God and Father
of Our Lord Jesus Christ**

19A

The Holy Trinity

Upper section

The Mystery of the Holy Trinity

 There is only *one God*, Genesis 1:1; Deuteronomy 6:4; Isaiah 42:8 (***symbol for God***).

 There are *three Persons* in that one God: Father, Son, and Holy Spirit, Matthew 28:19; 2 Corinthians 13:14. **ILLUSTRATION 19A** depicts the three Persons of the Trinity by symbols traditionally assigned to them—*Father:* ***Creative hand of God;*** *Son:* ***Servant-King, cross, open tomb, rising arrow;*** *Holy Spirit:* ***dove.***

 Although each Person is fully God (***equal sign***), each Person is distinct (***equal sign canceled out***) from the other two Persons, Matthew 25:34; John 16:12–15.

 In the New Testament, we read that the Father "begat" the Son (Hebrews 1:5; 5:5) and that the Father and the Son "sent" the Spirit, John 14:16; 16:7. These terms do not mean that one Person existed before another. They point to distinctions between the Persons, not to events in the sweep of time. (The term "begat" denotes that God the Father caused the Virgin Mary to conceive—miraculously.)

The Works of the Trinity

 Creation (***Creative hand of God***)*:* God the Father created all things, still owns them, and sustains what He has made and owns.

 Redemption (buy back, save, rescue): The work of God's Son, Jesus the Messiah, is designated by the ***Servant-King carrying His cross*** and an ***open tomb with rising arrow*** to remind us that Jesus' *life*, *death*, *resurrection*, and *ascension* was a serving, saving action, Matthew 1:21, Philippians 2:5–11. Jesus came to save us from slavery to sin and from the punishment we deserve in eternity, Romans 3:28.

 Sanctification (make holy): The Holy Spirit leads people to believe in Jesus the Messiah as Savior and Lord, and inspires and empowers them to do the things Jesus would lead them to believe and do if Jesus were still present in human form and visibly active on earth, John 16:12–15. The Holy Spirit perpetuates Jesus' completed mission and ministry.

The Bible does not distinguish sharply between the Persons of the Trinity. For example, Trinitarian terms overlap in Romans 8:9,10. Nor does the Bible divide the works of the Trinity into watertight compartments; it teaches that the Triune God creates, redeems, and sanctifies, 2 Corinthians 5:19.

Lower section

The doctrine of the Trinity is a mystery we cannot understand. However, although we cannot understand the multiple yet unified nature of the Trinity, we are called to praise the three Persons of the one Triune God for their gracious works, or *functions*, on our behalf (***persons in posture of praise***). For example, in Ephesians 1:3–14, Paul refers to the person and work of the Father in vv. 3–6, the Son in vv. 7–12, and the Spirit in vv. 13,14—and concludes each section with a summons to praise.

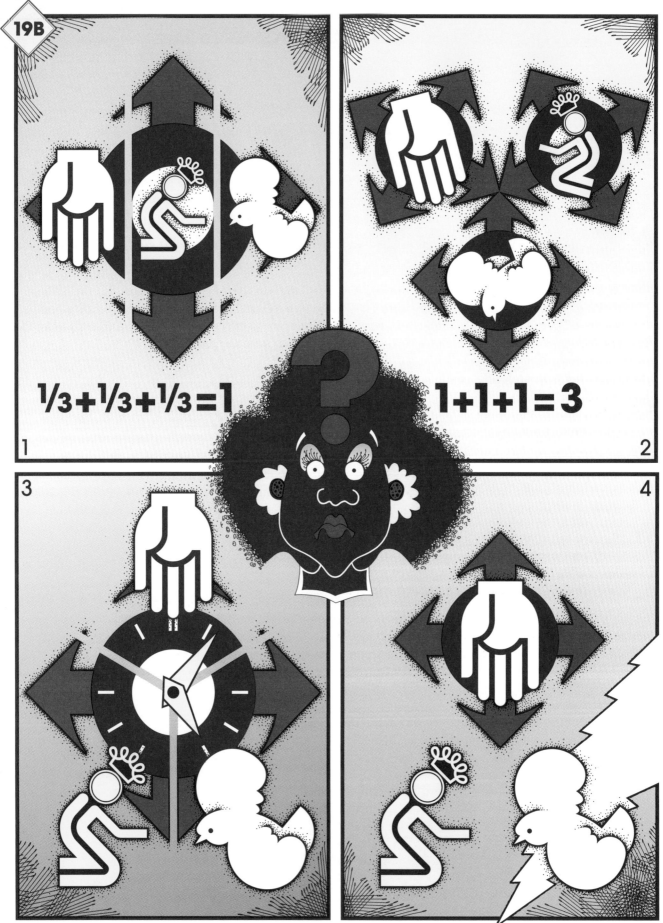

Over the centuries, some people have believed and taught incorrect ideas about the Trinity. The four frames in **ILLUSTRATION 19B** depict some of these ideas. In this illustration, the ***Creative hand of God*** refers to God the Father as creator, the ***Servant-King*** to Jesus the Messiah, and the ***dove*** to the Holy Spirit.

 Some people divide God into three equal portions, and think of each Person as one third of God (the Trinity by *fractions*, by *division*).

 Some speak as though each Person is a separate god (the Trinity by *addition*). However, the Bible teaches that there are three Persons within the one God, not three gods.

 Some suggest that the one God simply acts in different ways at different times (***clock face divided into three sections***)—sometimes as the Father, sometimes as the Son, and sometimes as the Holy Spirit (the Trinity by *shift work*).

 Some say that the Father alone is God, that at some point in time (creation, or the conception of Jesus) the Father created the Son, and that the Holy Spirit (***dove***) is merely God's power (***lightning***) at work in the world.

Although we can explain what the Bible teaches about the Trinity, we cannot understand the mystery of the Trinity. The Trinity can only be *believed* and *praised*.

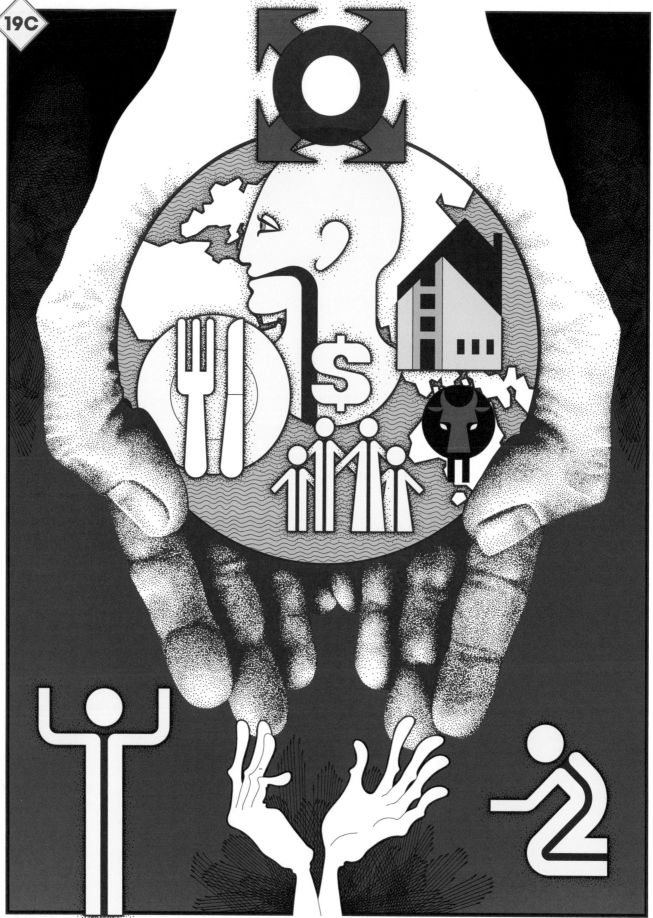

19C

© H. N. Wendt 2004

The structure and message of the Apostles' Creed is better understood when it is set out as follows:

I Believe in God:

 God the Father Almighty, Maker of Heaven and Earth.

 God the Son, Jesus Christ our Lord.

 God, the Holy Spirit.

ILLUSTRATION 19C shows several truths about the first of these three statements, often referred to as the *First Article* of the Apostles' Creed.

GOD MADE, OWNS, AND CARES FOR CREATION

In **ILLUSTRATION 19C**, the **symbol for God** is superimposed on a depiction of **God's hands** holding **Planet Earth**. On Planet Earth are symbols of things God creates and provides to make a meaningful life possible for us. God places these things into our frail human hands (**hands**, *lower center*).

These details remind us that:

◆ God *made* the universe, and all within it, Genesis 1; Job 38:1–21.

◆ God *continues to own* the universe, and all within it. In Genesis 1:26, God gives Adam and Eve *dominion over*, not *ownership of*, the created order. See also Deuteronomy 8. *1 & 6 →7*

◆ God *supplies our needs* (but not *greeds!*) on a personal, family, community, and vocational level, Psalm 104, 145:16.

GOD SEEKS A RESPONSE FROM US

◆ We are to thank and praise God, Psalm 103:1–5, 118:1 (**person in posture of praise**, *lower left*). The issue at stake is not *God's ego*, but *our welfare—our sense of trust and peace*.

◆ God wants us to serve and obey Him, Psalm 100:1,2; Deuteronomy 6:4,5; Matthew 4:10; 22:34–40 (**servant figure**, *lower right*). When we trust and obey God—and when we care and share with our local, national, and world communities—peace and harmony prevail.

In the first Beatitude, Jesus says, "Blessed are the poor in spirit, for theirs is the kingdom of heaven," Matthew 5:3. These words might well be translated, "Blessed are those who know they are beggars before God." Everything beggars receive comes from outside themselves as a result of someone else's kindness. In kindness, God places into our hands all we need to support life. We merely receive. What beggars we are!

The Bible teaches that God made and owns creation and us. More people would understand this if two words were added to the First Article of the Apostles' Creed: "I believe in God the Father Almighty, Maker *and Owner* of heaven and earth." The challenge in our needy world is not to urge people to *give more*, but to inspire and equip them to *rob less*. The problem in our needy world is not *God's providing;* the problem is *human dividing*. People prefer to *keep for themselves* rather than *share with others*.

God Is For Us!

The numbers correspond to those in **ILLUSTRATION 19D**

Upper section

 In the *human* realm, when two people are on bad terms (***lightning flashes between two people with angry faces***) and fighting one another...

 ...both need to change inwardly and outwardly if they are to be *reconciled to one another* (*restored to fellowship with one another*), and if peace is to prevail (***lightning flashes change to arrows that denote love and service; angry faces change to smiling faces***).

Lower section

 In the *divine-human* realm, things are different. God is already on good terms with humanity. God does not need to change or be reconciled to humanity. In Jesus, God is for us, Romans 8:1,31 (***arrow depicting God's love passing through Jesus' cross to a person***).

However, the person depicted appears disinterested in God, and angry with God. The heart of the divine-human problem is that humanity is not reconciled to God (***lightning flash from man to God***). This grieves God (***God is depicted with a concerned face, and a tear flowing from an eye***). Furthermore, when people are not reconciled to God, they are not reconciled to others (***male and female persons in posture of indifference, symbols for sin***).

 God appeals to humanity to be reconciled to God and to receive in faith what He offers through Jesus' atoning death (***cross***). *When people come to faith in Jesus as Savior and Lord, their hearts and lives change* (***man now has a smiling face; arrow pointing to God denotes love and service***). The change in the person causes God joy (***God is depicted with a smiling face***). People reconciled to God now serve each other (***male and female persons in posture of praise, arrows pointing to neighbor***).

The Bible does not offer advice about how to reconcile God to us. God does not need to be reconciled to us—we need to be reconciled to God. *God is for us!* God met the first sin with forgiveness, and continues to meet all sin with forgiveness. Although God never treats sin lightly, God has already dealt with the sin of humanity by letting its consequences fall on Jesus. Paul puts it this way:

> *In Christ God was reconciling the world to Himself, not counting their trespasses against them.*
> (2 Corinthians 5:19)

The Bible does not give us advice about how we can make God love us—*God already does!* Furthermore, **when we come to faith in what God has already done for us, God calls us to show our love for God by loving other people.**

Upper section

❶ The Jewish rabbis (teachers) taught that God gave humanity's first parents *two* commandments; they were to serve God and to serve each other, Exodus 20:1–3; Leviticus 19:18. Adam and Eve sinned, and eventually God wiped out humanity, preserving only Noah and his three sons (Shem, Ham, and Japheth), and their respective wives.

❷ According to rabbinic tradition, God gave Noah *seven* commandments. "The commandments of Noah," which were understood to apply to all humanity, were the following: (1) The practice of equity. Prohibitions against: (2) Blaspheming the Name of God, (3) Idolatry, (4) Immorality, (5) Bloodshed, (6) Robbery, (7) Eating an uncooked limb torn from an animal.

❸ After God rescued the Israelites from Egypt in the Exodus, God made a covenant with them at Sinai. In this covenant, God gave them the Ten Commandments, plus 603 additional commandments. The Ten Commandments are given in Exodus 20:1–17, and repeated in Deuteronomy 5:6–21 with minor variations. The 603 additional commandments are given in Exodus, Leviticus, Numbers, and Deuteronomy. *Judaism insists, and rightly so, that these 613 commandments were given only to the Israelites and their descendants, the Jews.*

❹ After those taken into exile in Babylon in 597 and 587 B.C. began returning to Judah and Jerusalem in 538 B.C., they began developing "oral traditions" to supplement and explain the laws written in the Pentateuch, the first five Old Testament books. Some argued that God had whispered these to Moses, who memorized them and passed them on to Joshua, who passed them on to the elders, who finally passed them on to the members of the postexilic Great Assembly. These oral traditions were finally written down about A.D. 200 in the *Mishnah*. Additional collections of oral traditions were made in writings known as the *Tosefta* and *Gemara*.

❺ Jesus joined *loving God* to *loving neighbor*, Mark 12:28–34.

❻ Christians still today debate how the Ten Commandments should be numbered: Four to God and six to neighbor? Or, three to God and seven to neighbor?

❼ Jesus gives His followers only *one* commandment, "Copy Me!" (John 13:1–13,34,35). Jesus the Messiah teaches and models what Christians are to believe *and do*. Any Old Testament commandment repeated in the New Testament is merely a commentary on Jesus' one commandment. **Like Jesus, Christians are to use life to glorify God and serve others.**

Lower section

The illustration summarizes how God's children are to serve each other in the spirit of Jesus. It is based on commandments 4–10, as some Christian communities list them. The commandments define our duties to others. God wants us to:

4 establish God-pleasing *parent-child relationships in families*.

5 protect and care for our neighbor's *body*.

6 protect and enrich our neighbor's *marriage*.

7 protect our neighbor's *possessions*.

8 protect our neighbor's *reputation*.

9,10 avoid *coveting*. Here we ask God to protect us from living merely to get and enjoy things, and from manipulating others for our own advantage.

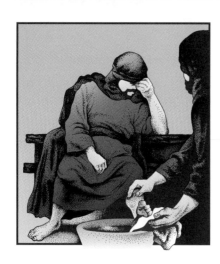

19A The Bible reveals the true and only God, the Triune God, in whom there are three Persons, Father, Son, and Holy Spirit. We cannot understand this mystery. However, we are to praise this Triune God for making us, redeeming us, and bringing us to faith in, and obedience to, Jesus the Messiah.

19B Human attempts to explain the Trinity are inadequate, and at times have resulted in confused and false teaching.

19C The Triune God made us, and graciously provides us with what God knows we need to sustain meaningful physical and spiritual life. God's will is that we respond to God's grace and goodness by living to thank and praise Him, and to serve and obey Him.

19D God revealed His will to ancient Israel through the commandments given at Sinai and during the wilderness wanderings. Jesus welded the service of God inseparably to the service of neighbor, and lived out what He taught. Jesus' life is our model for life.

19E The Bible does not tell us how to persuade God to love and forgive us. The Bible states that God already loves us, and has already forgiven us "in Christ"—and urges us to be reconciled to God in faith and life.

THE DIVINE DRAMA

OUR NARRATIVE

UNIT 20

Jesus the Messiah

20A

TODAY

FINAL APPEARING

The biblical teachings about Jesus the Messiah are profound and challenging. Even so, the Bible empowers us to come to joyous and victorious faith in Jesus as Savior, Lord, and Messiah.

ILLUSTRATION 20A builds on the symbol for the Trinity used in **ILLUSTRATION 19A**. From the lower left circle of the Trinity triangle (in which is the *Servant-King carrying His cross*), a *short arrow points down* to what the Bible teaches about Jesus' *person*, and *another arrow points upward* to what the Bible teaches about Jesus' *work*.

Lower section

The Person of Jesus (Savior) Christ (Messiah)

◆ The lower portion of **ILLUSTRATION 20A** depicts the profound truth that in Jesus the Messiah, that which is fully God (John 20:28; 1 John 5:20) united itself with that which is fully human—but sinless, Luke 2:7; John 1:14.

◆ Jesus' *deity* or *divine nature* is depicted by the *yellow section*, with an *arrow pointing backward and forward*—to indicate that *Jesus is the eternal God, without beginning and without end*, Hebrews 13:8; John 8:58 ("I AM"; see Exodus 3:14). To the left is the *symbol for God*. Jesus, the eternal second Person of the Trinity existed before creation (*Creative hand of God*, *symbols of creation*), and will always exist.

◆ Halfway along the yellow section is a *manger*, a symbol of Jesus' birth—that event in which God clothed Himself in flesh. To the right of the manger is a *blue section* signifying Jesus' *human nature*. This union of the divine and the human *began* when Jesus was conceived and born of the Virgin Mary, Matthew 1:18–25. Jesus *remains true man* as well as *true God today*, will show Himself as true-God/true-man at His *final appearing*, and will remain true-God/true-man to all eternity. The *question mark* serves to remind us that although Jesus *will reappear* at the end of history, we do not know *when* that event will take place.

Upper section

The Work of Jesus the Messiah

The numbers correspond to those in the upper section.

 Jesus, the Messianic King (*Servant-King*), lived the life of an obedient servant, totally dedicated to doing the will of His heavenly Father (*arrow going up to symbol for God linked to arrow pointing to neighbor*), 2 Corinthians 5:21; Galatians 4:4,5. Jesus served a sinful humanity (*person in posture of indifference, symbol for sin*), subject to death and condemnation (*tombstone with skull*).

 Jesus the Messiah finally surrendered Himself to crucifixion (*cross*) and burial (*tomb*) to endure the punishment the world deserves for its sin, 1 John 3:8; 2 Timothy 2:10; Romans 5:19.

 God raised Jesus from the dead (*open tomb*) to vindicate (to say "Yes!" to) Jesus' Messiahship, and to declare victory and authority over death and the grave, 1 Corinthians 15:51–57.

 In His ascension (*arrow rising into cloud*), Jesus did not *withdraw* His presence but *transformed* it. Jesus remains among us through the Holy Spirit (*dove; cloud of the divine presence*).

All that Jesus accomplished, He did *for us*. As the God-Man, Jesus was the *representative for the human race* who lived the life we were meant to live, *but cannot*, and suffered the death we deserve to suffer, *so that we need not*. In grace, God offers us all that Jesus was, is, and accomplished to possess as our very own. We receive and lay hold of God's gracious saving gifts in faith.

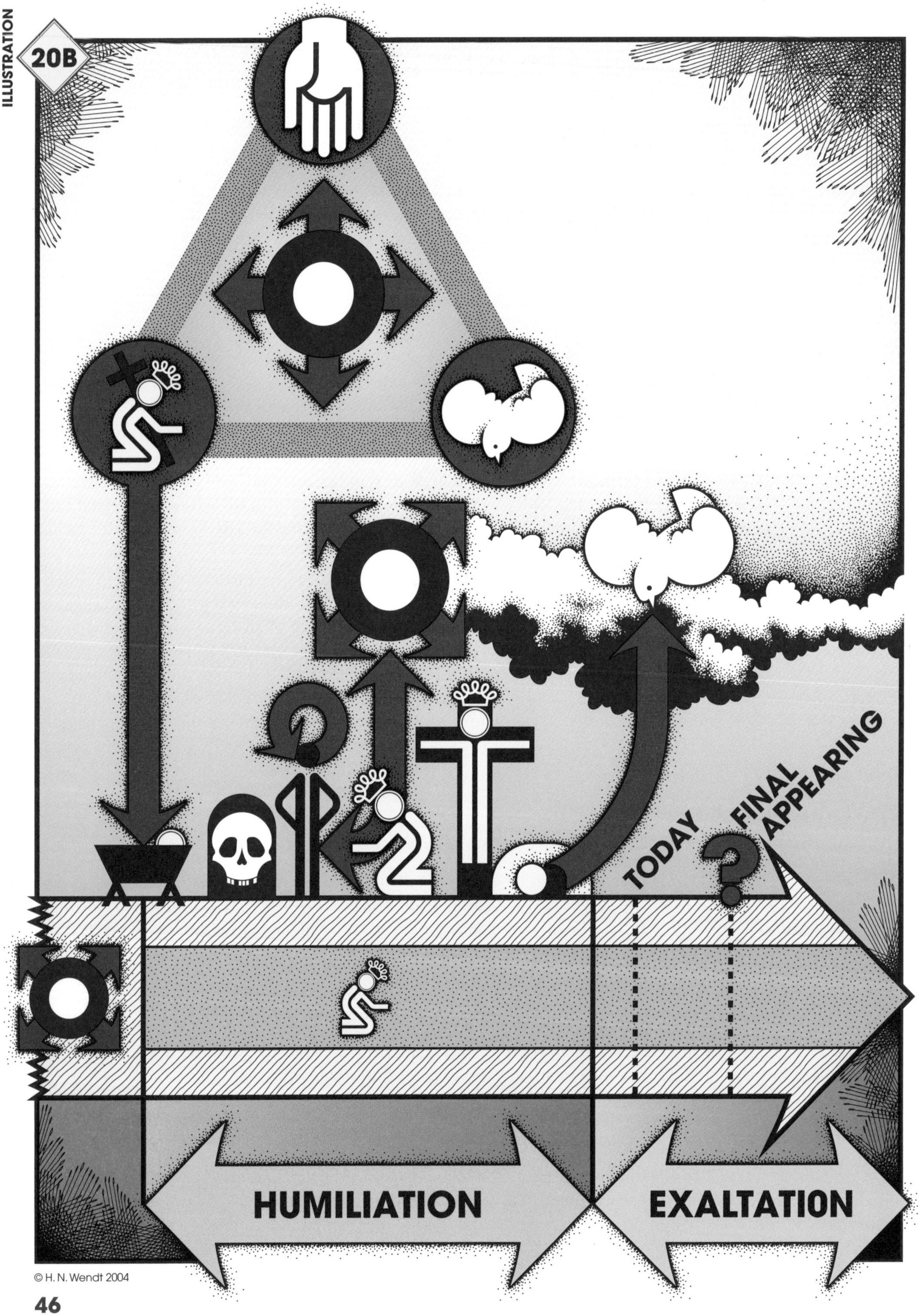

HUMILIATION

EXALTATION

TODAY

FINAL APPEARING

© H. N. Wendt 2004

The God-Man abused by humanity? The God-Man crucified? If Jesus really was God and Man in one Person, why did He permit these things to happen? The New Testament answers these questions with references to what some speak of as Jesus' *humiliation* and *exaltation*. **ILLUSTRATION 20B** draws on **ILLUSTRATION 20A** to convey its message.

HUMILIATION *(from conception and birth to death and burial)*

The period from Jesus' conception until the moment prior to His return to life in the tomb might be defined as Jesus' *humiliation*. This term does not mean that Jesus walked around boasting of His humility—in the spirit of Uriah Heep in Charles Dickens' *David Copperfield*, "I'm so 'umble, Mr. Davey—so 'umble." Rather, it signifies:

◆ During His earthly ministry, Jesus did not cease to be God, or become any less God. Jesus remained fully God and fully Man throughout His ministry, and does so still today (***Servant-King on blue section of arrow***). However, during His earthly ministry, Jesus did not always or fully use His divine powers, but humbled Himself, Philippians 2:4–11.

◆ What Jesus did throughout His life, Jesus did as the God-Man. Humanity had broken God's law (***person in posture of indifference***, ***symbol for sin***), and was subject to death, judgment, and condemnation (***tombstone with skull***). As the God-Man, Jesus kept the law perfectly *for sinful humans* who cannot keep it (***Servant-King, with arrow pointing up to symbol for God, and sideways to sinful humanity***). Furthermore, Jesus suffered what *sinful humanity* deserves to suffer for breaking God's law (***cross***). Jesus' dead body was placed into a ***tomb***.

◆ Because Jesus was *fully human*, He could enter the human scene, do what the human race was meant to do, and suffer what the human race deserves to suffer. Because Jesus was also fully God, what He accomplished was done for all humanity and can benefit all humanity, Galatians 4:4,5; 1 John 5:20; 2 Corinthians 5:15; 1 John 2:2.

EXALTATION *(beyond the resurrection to all eternity)*

◆ Beyond the resurrection (***open tomb***), Jesus, according to His *human nature*, fully and always makes use of the powers and qualities of His *divine nature*, Ephesians 1:19–23. For example, just as Jesus, according to His *divine nature*, has always been omnipresent (everywhere present), Jesus' *human nature* is now also omnipresent, Matthew 28:19,20.

◆ When Jesus rose from the earth into the cloud (*ascension*: ***arrow rising into cloud***, Acts 1: 1–9), the cloud symbolized the presence of God, Exodus 40:34–38; 1 Kings 8:10,11. In ascending, Jesus did not *withdraw* His physical presence—He *transformed* it. Jesus merely withdrew His visible, physical presence *from one place* so as to be present *everywhere in every place* invisibly.

◆ Jesus will one day reappear (***FINAL APPEARING***) to declare an end to history as we know it, and to usher in eternity, 2 Peter 3:1–13. We do not know when this grand finale to history will take place (***question mark***); only God knows, Mark 13:32.

Jesus did not cease to be true man at either His resurrection or His ascension. ***Jesus remains the God-Man. This truth invites us to approach Jesus in prayer with confidence.*** (Hebrews 4:14–16) ***He understands us completely, for He is still true man. Jesus is able to help us, for He is true God.***

20C

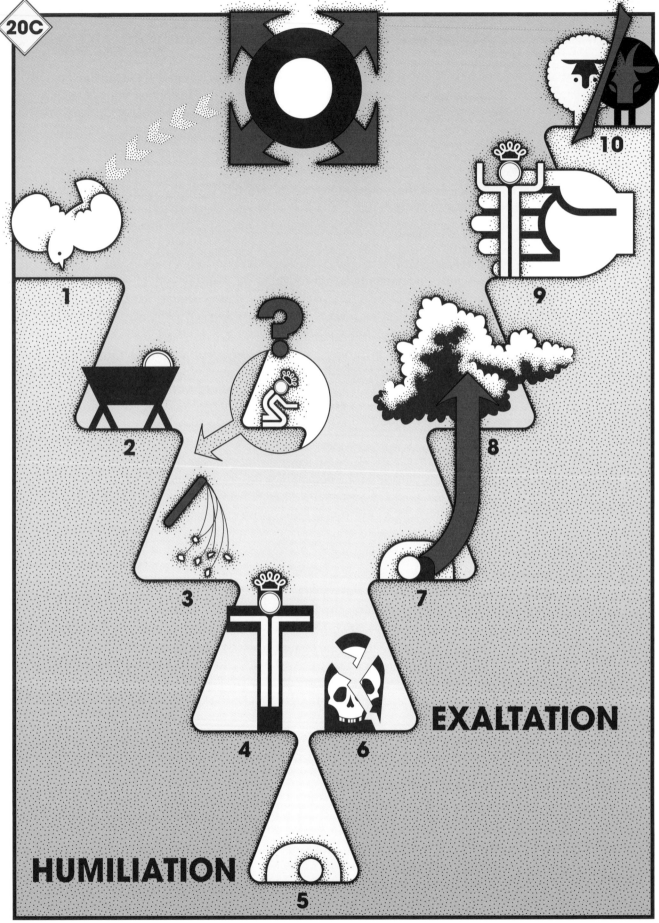

1

2

3

4

5

6

7

8

9

10

EXALTATION

HUMILIATION

Humiliation and Exaltation

ILLUSTRATION 20C expands on **ILLUSTRATION 20B** to depict the profound truths embedded in the short statements of the Apostles' Creed, and to relate them to Jesus' *humiliation* and *exaltation*. The Creed declares:

> *I believe in God the Father Almighty, Maker of Heaven and Earth, and in Jesus Christ, His only Son, our Lord, who…*

Steps Down in Jesus' HUMILIATION

 *was conceived by the Holy Spirit (**dove**, Luke 1:35),*

 *born of the Virgin Mary (**manger**, Matthew 1:20–23),*

 *suffered under Pontius Pilate (**scourge or whip**, John 18:28ff),*

 *was crucified (**cross**, John 19:18),*

 *died, and was buried (**sealed tomb**, John 19:30,42).*

Note the suggested additional "step" (beyond the reference to Jesus' birth) which proposes that a useful purpose would be served if the Creed also confessed, "*walked the way of a humble servant without limit.*"

Steps Up in Jesus' EXALTATION

 *He descended into hell (**shattered tombstone with skull**, 1 Peter 3:19–20),*

 *the third day He rose again from the dead (**open tomb**, Matthew 28:1–10),*

 *He ascended into heaven (**arrow rising into cloud**, Luke 24:50,51),*

 *and sits at the right hand of God the Father Almighty (**glorified Jesus at God's right hand**, Ephesians 1:19–22),*

 *from there He will come to judge the living and the dead (**sheep and goat separated**, John 5:28,29; Matthew 25:31–46).*

The Descent into hell

Step 6 in the *exaltation* segment does not mean that Jesus went to hell to suffer. Jesus' suffering for the sins of the world came to an end when He cried, "It is finished," John 19:30. Many interpret 1 Peter 3:19 to mean that, after returning to life, Jesus proclaimed His Lordship and authority also over the realm of the dead—often called *Sheol* in the Old Testament. (Note that the Sadducees believed that those who died went to the abode of the dead where they were cut off from God, and forgotten by God, Psalm 88.) Jesus' return to life took place before His descent into the abode of the dead. However, Jesus showed His disciples that He was alive *after* the descent—hence the order of the statements in the Apostles' Creed.

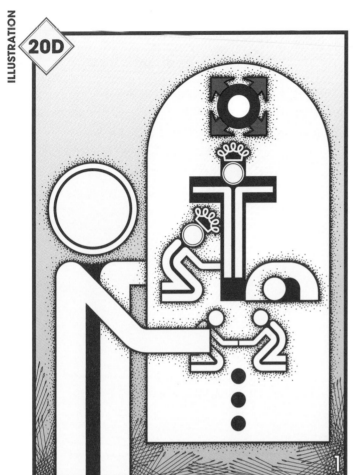

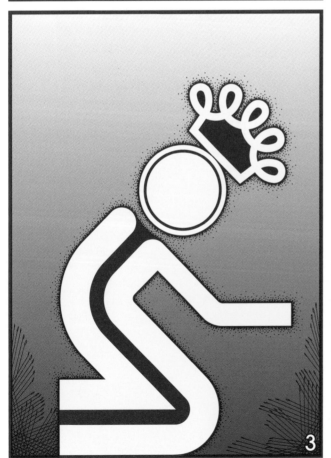

Aspects of Jesus' Work

It is traditional to speak of Jesus' work as *Prophet*, *Priest*, and *King*. **ILLUSTRATION 20D** adds a fourth—Jesus as *Wisdom*.

 Prophet

ILLUSTRATION 10A and the accompanying text in The **DIVINE DRAMA—The Biblical Narrative** discussed the role of the prophet in the life of Old Testament Israel. In the New Testament, Jesus proclaimed, or "forth-told," with His lips and life the mind and will of God, John 17:8. As God proclaimed the Old Covenant through Moses at Sinai, so Jesus established and proclaimed the New Covenant relationship between His Father and humanity, Jeremiah 31:31–34 and Hebrews 8:6–12; Exodus 24:3–11 and Mark 14:22–25. (*For the details on the **covenant symbol** depicted, see* **ILLUSTRATION 16B**, **DIVINE DRAMA—The Biblical Narrative**.)

 Priest

The Old Testament priests acted as mediators (go-betweens) between God and the Israelites in the worship and sacrificial rituals conducted at the shrines in ancient Israel. Jesus is now the mediator between God and humanity. Jesus sacrificed Himself as "the lamb of God who takes away the sin of the world," John 1:29,36; Hebrews 9:11–14; Romans 8:34. (***Servant Jesus wearing a priest's hat, and carrying his cross.***)

 King

The New Testament, especially the Gospels, refers frequently to Jesus' role as King, John 18:33–19:22. Jesus (***Servant-King***) rules a three-fold kingdom:

  a. Kingdom of *power:* Jesus has been declared Lord of the universe, Ephesians 1:20,21.

  b. Kingdom of *grace:* Jesus is Lord of God's people, the church, Ephesians 1:22.

  c. Kingdom of *glory:* Jesus is Lord of the world to come, Colossians 1:15–20.

 Wisdom

The Old Testament contains a number of books known as wisdom writings—Job, Proverbs, Ecclesiastes. Wisdom writers taught that there is a divine plan to the universe, and an answer to the meaning of life. This divine plan, this answer, can be discovered. People who know and build life around it possess wisdom, and are equipped to live in harmony with the Creator and creation.

In Matthew 12:42, Jesus refers to Himself as "One greater than Solomon." Little wonder that the wise men from the East paid homage to Jesus as the greatest of all wisdom teachers, Matthew 2:1–12; see also 1 Kings 4:34, 10:23–25. Jesus not only *taught* wisdom—His life was a *living display* of true wisdom. Paul also refers to Jesus as "the wisdom of God," 1 Corinthians 1:24. (***Servant Jesus, the lamp of wisdom above his head.***)

John 14:8–11 tells of a conversation between Jesus and His disciples. It might be summarized as follows:

> Philip: *Lord, show us what God is like. God is invisible. We cannot see God. If we could see God and know what He is like, we would find this very helpful.*

> Jesus: *I have been with you for quite some time, Philip, and you still do not know who I am? If you have seen me, you have seen the invisible Father. I make Him visible through my Person, words, and works.*

 What Jesus teaches in John 14 is taught elsewhere in the New Testament:

> *Jesus the Messiah is the image of the invisible God.* (Colossians 1:15)

> *No one has ever seen God; it is God the only Son, who is close to the Father's heart, who has made him known.* (John 1:18)

> *The god of this world has blinded the minds of the unbelievers, to keep them from seeing the light of the Gospel of the glory of Christ, who is the image of God.* (2 Corinthians 4:4)

> *He [Jesus] is the reflection of God's glory and the exact imprint of God's very being.* (Hebrews 1:3)

 ILLUSTRATION 20E depicts the truths expressed above. The *eye* in the illustration is *our* eye. When we look at what the New Testament teaches about Jesus' visible Person, life, teaching, and ministry (***Servant-King carrying His cross***), we learn more about the invisible God (***cloud depicting the presence and glory of God***).

As Jesus was on earth, the Father is now. As Jesus treated people then, so the Father treats us now. As Jesus' disposition was, the Father's disposition is. As Jesus was and is and always will be, so the Father was and is and always will be. Jesus and the Father are one, John 17:11,20–22. **To know Jesus is to know the invisible God.**

 The Gospels offer many insights into Jesus' personality:

a. His compassion in dealing with outcasts, Matthew 8:1–4.
b. His kindness toward those burdened by sin, Luke 7:48–50.
c. His boldness when confronted by the demonic, Mark 1:25.
d. His composure when dealing with opponents, John 8:42–47.
e. His loving patience with confused disciples, John 21:15–17.
f. His courage in the face of imminent death, Mark 10:32–34.

When we understand how Jesus related to people during His earthly ministry, we understand how God relates to us today.

1

2

In Ephesians 1:19–23, Paul says the almighty power of God that raised Jesus from the dead is also at work in the hearts and lives of those who believe in Jesus. Paul goes on to say that after the Father raised Jesus from the dead, "God seated Him at His right hand in the heavenly places," 1:20. What does this statement mean?

In the ancient world, the ownership of a nation or city was assigned to a particular god. However, that god did not rule the nation or city directly, but used an earthly ruler as the representative to do so. Accordingly, in statues and illustrations, the earthly representative was depicted standing at the god's right hand; to stand at the right hand was to be in the position of authority.

Paul's point in Ephesians 1:19–23 is that after the Father raised Jesus from the dead, *He gave Him the place of honor and authority in the universe.* Jesus rules the universe for His Father, and does it with the welfare of His people in mind, "for the church," 1:22.

Upper section

> The **symbol for God** is superimposed on a **throne**. The **glorified Jesus** the Messiah is at God's "**right hand**," the place of authority.

Lower section

> The lower section of the illustration depicts **a corner of the universe**, with **Planet Earth** and **phases of the moon enlarged**.
>
> In the upper left, Jesus' new community, the new and true Israel, gathers around its Lord, Jesus the Messiah (**circle of small circles around the Servant-King carrying His cross**).

The truths depicted in **ILLUSTRATION 20F** are a source of great comfort to Christians. Jesus the Messiah has authority over the universe, the church, and our lives. We know the Person "in charge," and we know that He is for us, Romans 8:1. We can have an inner peace in all we do, Philippians 4:4–7.

At times, history seems to be "just one fool thing after another." Even so, the Bible insists that Jesus guides all history so that we, Jesus' brothers and sisters, are given the opportunity to live, not necessarily *comfortably*, but *usefully*—in a way that reflects Jesus' attitude towards the Father, the created order, and humanity.

In Ephesians 1:22, Paul writes:

> *And He* [God] *has put all things under his* [Jesus'] *feet and has made him the head over all things for the church.*

Ancient practices color Paul's statement. In the ancient Near East, a king had the faces or figures of conquered enemies carved or embroidered onto his footstool, and then placed his feet on it. The implication was obvious; the king had authority over those whose images appeared on his footstool.

ILLUSTRATION 20G depicts *Jesus' feet resting on a footstool*. On Jesus' feet are symbols of the *Servant-King*, a *cross*, an *open tomb*, and a *rising arrow* symbolizing Jesus' resurrection and ascension. Above these is a *dove*, a symbol for the Holy Spirit.

The six symbols on the footstool are (reading clockwise from upper left corner):

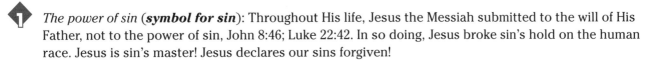 *The power of sin* (*symbol for sin*): Throughout His life, Jesus the Messiah submitted to the will of His Father, not to the power of sin, John 8:46; Luke 22:42. In so doing, Jesus broke sin's hold on the human race. Jesus is sin's master! Jesus declares our sins forgiven!

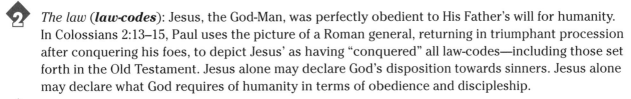 *The law* (*law-codes*): Jesus, the God-Man, was perfectly obedient to His Father's will for humanity. In Colossians 2:13–15, Paul uses the picture of a Roman general, returning in triumphant procession after conquering his foes, to depict Jesus' as having "conquered" all law-codes—including those set forth in the Old Testament. Jesus alone may declare God's disposition towards sinners. Jesus alone may declare what God requires of humanity in terms of obedience and discipleship.

Judgment and condemnation (*gavel*): Jesus' dealings with, and victory over, all law-codes, including those set forth in the Old Testament, destroyed their authority to judge and condemn those who put their trust in Him, Romans 8:1,2,33,34.

Satan (*satanic face*): Jesus' ministry throughout His life on earth was a battle with Satan and his realm. Jesus won the battle, Mark 3:22–27; 1 John 3:8.

The heavenly powers (*crown with the astrological symbols*): The reference is to terms Paul uses in Ephesians 1:21, 6:12; Colossians 1:16; Romans 8:38,39. In these passages, Paul states that Jesus has authority over every so-called power in the universe. (Further reference will be made to these powers in Unit 30.)

Death (*tombstone with skull*): Jesus is Lord over death. The grave must obey when Jesus finally commands it to yield up its victims, Luke 7:11–17; John 5:25–29; 11:25,26,43,44.

Paul vividly sums up Jesus' Lordship when he writes:

> *Therefore God also highly exalted Jesus, and gave Him a name that is above every name, so that at the name of Jesus every knee should bend, in heaven and on earth and under the earth, and every tongue should confess that Jesus Christ is Lord, to the glory of God the Father.* (Philippians 2:9–11)

20A At Jesus' conception, God united Himself with humanity in one person, Jesus the Messiah. As the God-Man, Jesus lived the life we were meant to live but cannot, and died the death we deserve to die so that we need not.

20B Although from His conception to His burial, Jesus was true God as well as true man, He did not *always or fully* use His power as God (*humiliation*). However, Jesus has *always* done so after returning to life in the tomb (*exaltation*).

20C The Apostles' Creed refers to both Jesus' *humiliation* and *exaltation* (*humiliation:* from "was conceived by the Holy Spirit" to "was crucified, died, and was buried"; *exaltation:* from "He descended into hell" to "to judge the living and the dead").

20D The New Testament speaks of Jesus' roles as Prophet, Priest, King, and Wisdom.

20E Although we cannot see God in His glory and majesty, Jesus' life and teachings reveal His Father's heart and character.

20F After God raised Jesus from the dead, God gave Jesus authority over the created order and the course of history. Jesus directs all things so that His Father is glorified—often in ways humanity does not readily understand.

20G The New Testament states that Jesus has authority over all powers and authorities in the universe, and directs them to the glory of God and for the welfare of God' people. Christians find great comfort in knowing that Jesus is both Savior and Lord, and that Jesus is *for us* in time and eternity.

THE DIVINE DRAMA®

OUR NARRATIVE

UNIT 21
The Holy Spirit

21A

Jesus and the Spirit

The Relationship of the Persons

 God united His deity with humanity when Mary conceived, Luke 1:31. The God-man, Jesus the Messiah, lived the life of a sinless Servant (**Servant-King**), was crucified, died (**cross**), and was buried (**tomb**). Jesus' "glory" was very different from worldly ideas of glory, in that He lived to serve others even to the point of giving away life. (Note John 19:30. After saying, "It is finished," Jesus bowed His head and *gave up His spirit*.)

 Jesus returned to life on Easter Sunday morning (**open tomb**), and eventually "was carried up into heaven," Luke 24:50,51 (**arrow rising into cloud**, *symbol of God's presence*, Exodus 19:9, 1 Kings 8:10). In ascending, Jesus did not *withdraw* His presence; He *transformed* it. Jesus is now present *everywhere in the universe* as the God-man.

 Although Jesus said that He would send the Holy Spirit to His disciples after He ascended (John 14:16; 16:7), Jesus also said that He Himself would come and abide with them (John 14:18), and that He and the Father would come and make their home with them, John 14:23. Jesus will remain with His people in every place until the close of the age, Matthew 28:20 (**arrow descends from cloud**).

 The triumphant Jesus continues His work through the Holy Spirit (**dove**) who speaks to humanity through the Holy Scriptures (**Bible**, *lower right*), Holy Baptism (**drop of water**), and His Holy Meal (**bread and cup**).

Jesus call His followers to reflect His glory throughout life in all they do by seeking to live as Jesus lived (*servanthood:* **Servant-King**). Jesus promises that eventually He will take them to share His glory in the presence of the Father, John 17:22–24 (**arrow at right rising into cloud**).

The Relationship of Their Work

 All three Persons of the Holy Trinity cooperate in the works of creation, redemption, and sanctification (see **ILLUSTRATION 19A**). Concerning the relationship between Jesus' work and that of the Holy Spirit, Jesus says:

> But the Advocate, the Holy Spirit, whom the Father will send in my name, will teach you everything, and remind you of all that I have said to you. (John 14:26)

> He [the Holy Spirit] will glorify Me, for He will take what is mine and declare it to you. All that the Father has is mine. For this reason I said that He will take what is mine and declare it to you. (John 16:14,15)

 The Holy Spirit continues to teach and accomplish what Jesus would seek to teach and accomplish if Jesus were still visibly among humanity. The Spirit continues to make known Jesus' saving work. Their work is one and inseparable.

 The Holy Spirit is like a director who takes his place at the side of the stage and repeatedly beckons the audience to direct its attention to the lead actor on center stage. The Holy Spirit points constantly to *Jesus*, urging all to watch *Jesus* that they might come to saving faith in *Him*. **The person who is most of the Holy Spirit is the person who is most of Jesus.**

Sinai and Pentecost

ILLUSTRATION 6E in **The DIVINE DRAMA—The Biblical Narrative** depicted the events that took place at Mt. Sinai, Exodus 19,20. Although the Bible describes God coming down to the top of Sinai, it does not describe God going back up into the heavens again. Rather, it says that God took up residence among the Israelites in the Tabernacle (Exodus 40:34–38) and later dwelt in their midst in the Jerusalem Temple, 1 Kings 8:10–13. The Old Testament outlines the history of a people who understood themselves as living in the presence of God.

There are parallels between the events of Sinai and the events of Pentecost as described in Acts 2 (compare **ILLUSTRATION 6E** in **The DIVINE DRAMA—The Biblical Narrative** with **ILLUSTRATION 21B**). In both, the community (*circle of people holding hands*) is gathered around a central Person. In **ILLUSTRATION 6E**, God's presence is symbolized by the storm cloud and lightning at the top of Sinai. In **ILLUSTRATION 21B**, the community is gathered around the risen Jesus and the Holy Spirit (*glorified Jesus*, *dove*). Fire-like tongues rest on each person's head, and the people hear a noise like a wind storm, Acts 2:1–3 (*tongues of fire and wind*, *upper section*). The events of Sinai and Pentecost are closely related.

◆ **Sinai**

God descended and took up residence among the Israelites whom He had rescued ("redeemed") from Egypt. God declared that He was their God and they were His people, made a covenant with them, gave them law-codes to direct their lives, and then led them from Sinai through the wilderness into the Promised Land.

◆ **Pentecost**

The victorious Jesus descended and took up residence among His new people. Jesus had already redeemed them through His life, death, and resurrection, and instructed them in the ways of discipleship. At Pentecost, Jesus fulfilled His promise to remain with them until the close of this age (Matthew 28:20), and to lead them through the wilderness of this life to the eternal Promised Land, John 10:11–16; 1 Peter 1:3–5.

A New People—A Renewed Mission

 God created Old Israel to be His special people and to bear witness to God among the nations, Genesis 12:1–3. Their obedience was to serve as a magnet to attract others to faith in God, Deuteronomy 4:6–8. They failed in their mission!

 The events of Pentecost are the culmination of God's plan to create a New Israel, a new people, whose mission was and is to bear witness to God among the nations, Acts 1:8.

 The festival of Pentecost had been observed for centuries prior to the events recorded in Acts 2. By Jesus' day, it had developed into a commemoration of the events at Sinai.

 The Pentecost described in Acts 2 witnessed the beginning of a *New Israel* which was formed to put right what went wrong in the life of *Old Israel*.

5 Today's worldwide Christian community is a continuation of the community that began in Jerusalem about 2,000 years ago. **God formed it, in grace, for a purpose: to make God known and to live in a manner that reflects God's original plan for humanity.**

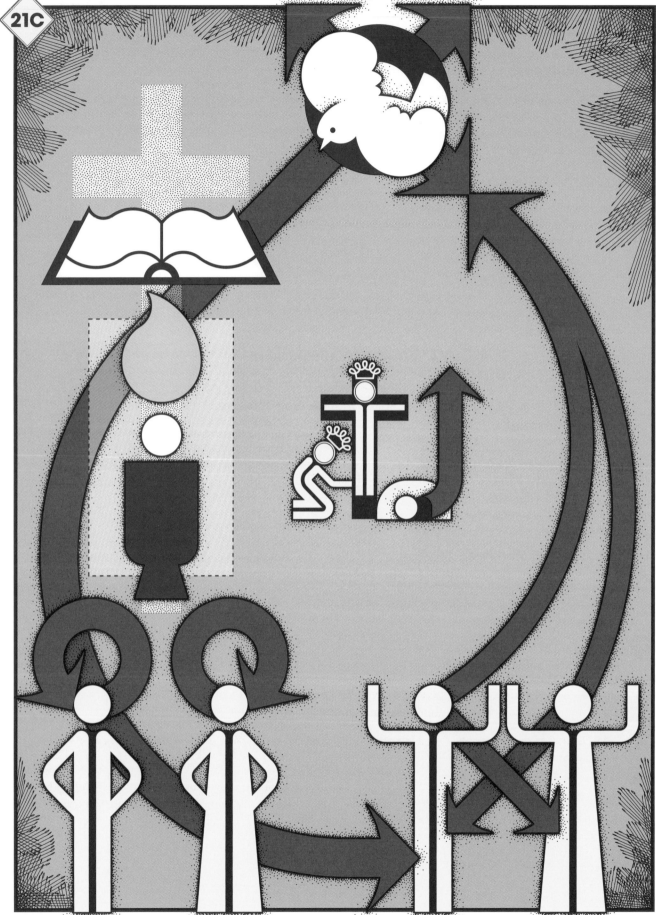

Although God's handiwork in creation reveals His power and wisdom, it does not reveal God's grace and forgiveness. Furthermore, God does not speak to us directly to reveal His heart and will; God reveals them to humanity through His Means of Grace.

What Are the Means of Grace?

 God's Means of Grace are the **Bible** (*upper left*), Holy Baptism (**drop of water**), and Holy Communion (or: Lord's Supper, Eucharist, Holy Meal; **bread and cup**).

 In **ILLUSTRATION 21C**, a **cross** passes through all three Means of Grace, for all three proclaim God's good news: God has rescued fallen humanity through the life, death, and resurrection of God's Son, Jesus the Messiah. The core of the message is the forgiveness of sins through faith in all that Jesus accomplished for us, which in turn calls us to "put off" our former sinful way of life and "put on" Jesus' way of life.

 The arrow that comes from the **symbol for God** and the Holy Spirit (**dove**) passes through the Means of Grace to the persons below. The **persons are in a posture of indifference** to God; they are subject to the power of sin (**symbols for sin**). God does not wait for them to first repent or reform before deciding to forgive them. By virtue of Jesus' saving life, death, and resurrection, God offers divine mercy and forgiveness to all people.

 Through the Means of Grace, God seeks not only to *redeem* (or rescue) fallen humanity, but also to *restore* people to God's original plan. God seeks to change people from their old way of life (*lower left*) to God's new way of life so that they live to praise and serve God and serve others (**male and female persons in posture of praise**, **arrows pointing to neighbor**) *lower right*). *Redemption* and *restoration* are to go hand in hand. The first is complete. The second continues to take place throughout life, Ephesians 4:17–24.

Note that some churches teach there are seven sacraments. Others speak of two main sacraments and five sacramental signs.

What is a Sacrament?

A sacrament:

- Is a sacred act commanded and instituted by Jesus, Matthew 28:19,20; 26:26–28.
- Derives its power and authority from God speaking through God's Word (**Bible**).
- Employs a visible means for conveying its message (*Holy Baptism*, **drop of water**; *Holy Communion*, **bread and cup**. Some Christian groups use grape juice rather than fermented wine).
- Conveys a divine promise (1 Peter 3:21; Matthew 26:28), the forgiveness of sins.

All three Means of Grace convey the same basic message, "Your sins are forgiven!" The *Bible* conveys the message through words that we hear. *Holy Baptism* and *Holy Communion* convey the message through visible acts that touch our bodies.

We might refer to the three Means of Grace as God's *audible Word* (Bible), God's *adopting Word* (Holy Baptism), and God's *edible Word* (Holy Communion).

It is said that Martin Luther's dying words were, "What beggars we are!" He meant that whatever we humans are, whatever we possess, whatever truth we know of God's grace and will, whatever sincere obedience we render, are to be understood as gifts placed by God into the hands of undeserving beggars.

The Nature of the Spirit's Gift Package

In **ILLUSTRATION 21D**, the symbol for the Holy Spirit (*dove*) is placed on a symbol of *God's powerful hands* which offer the Spirit's *gift package* to the *weak, beggarly hands of fallen humanity* (*lower right*). Through this gift package, the Holy Spirit seeks to enlighten (*lamp*, *lower left*) those in the darkness of sin and death, Ephesians 5:8–11. The numbers below correspond to the numbers in the Spirit's gift package.

 The Holy Spirit gives us the *Bible*, God's teaching tool, 1 Corinthians 2:13.

 The Holy Spirit teaches us that we are in bondage to *sin* (Romans 6:20; *symbol for sin*), and therefore subject to *death* (Romans 6:23; *tombstone with skull*) and *judgment* (Romans 5:18; *sheep, goat*).

 The Holy Spirit teaches us about Jesus the Messiah's saving mission and ministry.

    a.   Jesus, the Messianic King, lived the life of a servant for us (*Servant-King*).

    b.   Jesus was crucified, died, and was buried for us. Jesus' *cross* was His throne.

    c.   Jesus rose from the dead (*open tomb*) and ascended into heaven (*rising arrow*).

    d.   Jesus will remain among us until the close of this age (*glorified Jesus*).

    e.   Jesus works through the Holy Spirit (*dove*) to teach us about His saving work for us.

 The Holy Spirit creates in our hearts the faith that accepts and clings to Jesus (as a *person clings to a life preserver; cord linking life preserver to Jesus' person and work;* see also **ILLUSTRATION 22F** and **ILLUSTRATION 22G**), Romans 10:14.

 The Holy Spirit empowers us to reflect Jesus' servant life (*servant figure*), John 13:12–15.

 The Holy Spirit keeps us in the faith so that we might receive Jesus' final "Welcome Home!" (Matthew 25:34; *glorified Jesus with arms extended in welcome*). See also 1 Peter 1:5.

 After the final "Welcome Home!" God's children will be given the crown of eternal life, Revelation 2:10 (*crown*).

Who Finds and Accepts Whom?

We should ask ourselves the following questions:

    ◆   *Who* gave me the Bible?

    ◆   *Who* brought me into contact with it?

    ◆   *Who* moved me to think about its message?

    ◆   *Who* brought me to faith in Jesus the Messiah?

    ◆   *Who* teaches me how Jesus wants me to live?

    ◆   *Who* empowers me to believe and do Jesus' will?

    ◆   *Who* enables me to persevere in faith and discipleship?

    ◆   *Who* makes it possible for me to receive eternal life?

The answer to each question is, "God, the Holy Spirit, does it all." We humans have no cause to boast.

21A The third Person of the Holy Trinity, the Holy Spirit, has one desire: to teach people about Jesus the Messiah and to draw them into a saving relationship with Him. The work of the risen Jesus and the work of the Holy Spirit are one and inseparable.

21B During the Pentecost events outlined in Acts 2, the risen Jesus came mightily among the disciples to equip and empower them for His mission to the nations. The work of salvation accomplished in Jerusalem had to be proclaimed in Rome!

21C Still today, the Holy Spirit gathers people into Jesus' community—working through the Means of Grace: the Bible, Holy Baptism, and Holy Communion. Through these, the Holy Spirit declares to us the forgiveness of our sins, and restores us to God's original plan for life—to serve God and others.

21D Our pride tempts us to think that we help produce our faith and discipleship. However, mature reflection shows that the Holy Spirit does it all. We Christians remain beggars before God. The faith that trusts in Jesus as Savior and Lord is God's creation within us, and the service we render God and others is the result of God at work within us.

THE DIVINE DRAMA®

OUR NARRATIVE

UNIT 22

God's Grace—Human Response

22A

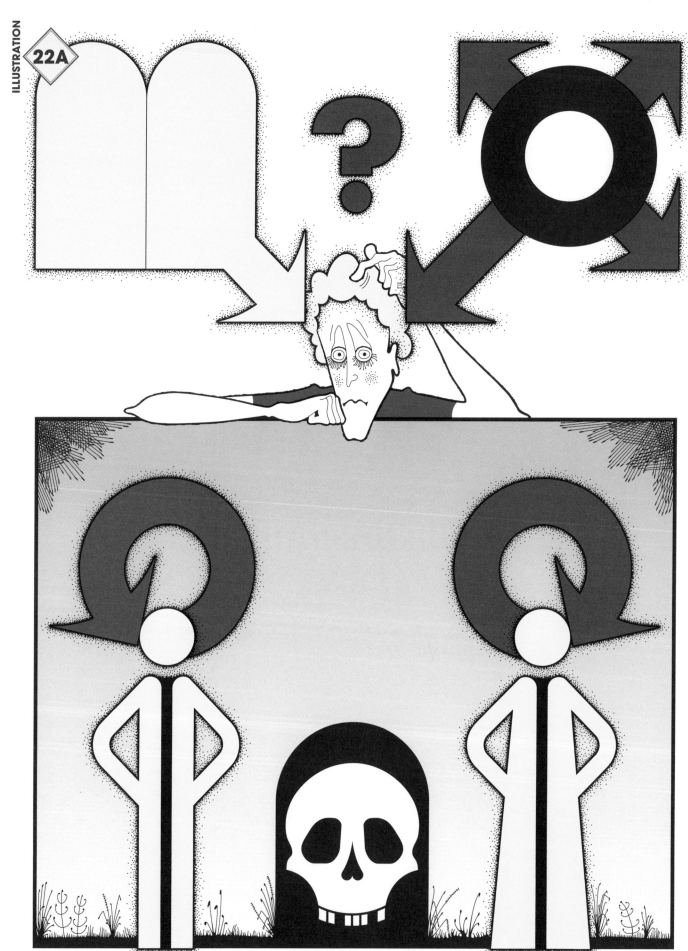

22A

After God created our first parents, they sinned. They no longer lived to serve God and others, but lived for themselves, Romans 6:12–14 (***male and female persons***, ***symbol for sin***, *lower section*). With sin came death, Romans 6:23 (***tombstone with skull***, *lower section*,). To what or to whom were they to look for help, for rescue? Because we too are "in Adam" (**ILLUSTRATION 18B**, Romans 5:12), to what are we to look for rescue? Do we look to our attempts to keep God's commandments (***law-codes***, *upper left*), or do we look to what God has done for us (***symbol for God***, *upper right*)?

The Human Solution

 How do you react to the following statement?

> *Soon after God made the universe and our first parents, God said to Adam and Eve, "I have some commandments for you. If you keep them, you can become my children."*

The statement is false.

 By nature, misguided humanity thinks obeying the commandments restores fellowship with God. To believe and do this is to put God's commandments to a use God never intended. No set of rules, laws, or commandments can put matters right between God and humanity—whether they be the commandments from the Bible, or other laws and commandments, Romans 3:19,20. The human solution is *not a solution*. It is based on the idea that *people* can establish fellowship with God by *what they themselves do*.

 The commandments were not given to *affect*, establish, or bring about a relationship with God. They were given to serve as guidelines for *reflecting* a relationship with God—a relationship God had already established.

The Divine Solution

 The solution to the problem must come from God. God insists on being entirely the *giver* in the sphere of salvation. People can merely *receive* what God *gives*.

 To what, then, do we look for salvation? To a *program*—obedience to commandments? Or to a *Person*? The answer is obvious. We must always look to a Person, to what God has done for us and offers us freely in grace through Jesus the Messiah.

When God revealed divine truth to humanity, God did not provide the biblical writers with a new set of heaven-designed words to express that truth. God guided them to use earthly words to express God's truth. The Bible uses a number of such words and terms to refer to sin. **ILLUSTRATION 22B** depicts four of these words. (The numbers below correspond to those in the illustration.)

1 *Original sin* refers to the fallen human nature we have inherited from Adam. *Original* sin gives rise to *actual* sins. In Greek, the word the Bible uses for *sin* means to *miss the mark, to miss a target or a road*. Frame 1 shows Sylvester **firing arrows** at a **target**, with a **servant figure** at its center. None of the arrows strikes the bull's-eye of the target. Sylvester's aim is misdirected by sin (**symbol for sin on his extended arm**).

2 Frame 2 depicts a second word: *trespass*. It means *to walk in forbidden places*, Ephesians 2:1. The illustration shows Sylvester walking where he is being told he should not walk—in *the region of sin* (**symbol for sin**).

3 *Transgress* means *to go beyond a limit, to cross over a line*. Frame 3 shows Sylvester **rushing beyond the "safety line" towards a cliff**.

4 Frame 4 shows Sylvester with **a raised arm holding a rock**. On his arm is the **symbol for sin**. He is preparing to throw the rock at God's commandments (**law-codes**), on which are **two servant figures facing each other**. The illustration depicts several words that denote contempt for God's law: *revolt, rebellion, defiance of God, lawlessness*, 1 Timothy 1:9,10.

The Sin Thermometer

On the left side of **ILLUSTRATION 22C** is a ***thermometer***. Its bulb resembles the ***symbol for sin***. To the right of the thermometer are ***three people engaged in different actions***. Which action poses the biggest threat to the work of God's Kingdom? Which of the three is the *hottest sin*?

Upper section

Eyes on Target

A gangster walks into a restaurant and shoots some people. He knows his actions are wrong, and flees from the scene. Everyone knows organized crime is wrong.

Middle section

Eyes on Money

In many countries, people are pressured to accumulate money. "Make what you can, 'can' what you make, and sit on the lid!" Those who progress from rags to riches are applauded as successful. Generally speaking, people around the world are manipulated into buying what they do not need, with money they do not have, in order to impress people who do not care.

It is not wrong to *have* money. What matters is *how we get it*, and *what we do with it when we have it*. The Bible does not say that *money* is the root of all evils, but that *the love of money* is the root of all evils, 1 Timothy 6:10. However, the drive to get money and the urge to spend it *for self* plunge many into sin.

Lower section

Eyes on Personal Pampering

It is not wrong to watch TV; people need time for leisure and relaxation. If we do not come apart and rest awhile, there is danger that we will "come apart," Mark 6:31.

Even so, the illustration depicts what is perhaps the most dangerous situation of all. It is possible to fritter away life doing nothing *wrong*, but nothing *good*. People ask, "What *harm* am I doing?" God also asks, "What *good* are you doing?" We are not here to live *comfortably*, but *usefully*. We live usefully, not in order *to be saved*, but to show that we *have been saved*.

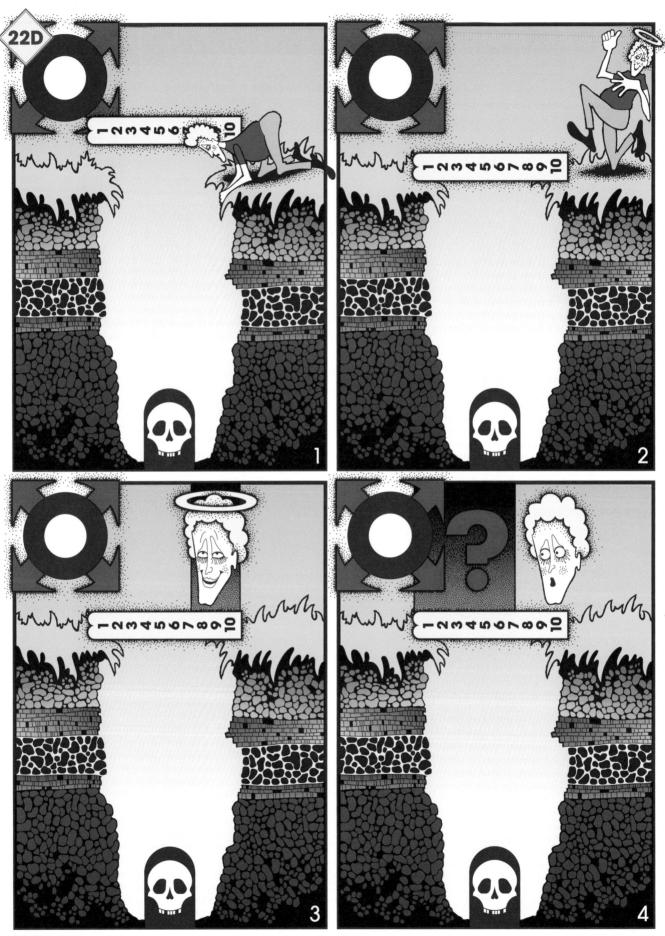

Done—Undone

In Isaiah 59:2, the prophet writes, "Your iniquities have made a separation between you and your God" (RSV). The *gulf* in **ILLUSTRATION 22D** depicts the separation between God and humanity. The numbers below refer to the four sections of the illustration.

1 Our sin has created a ***gulf between God and us***. God's ***commandments*** (which we have not kept and cannot keep) show the extent of the gulf. The existence of the gulf perplexes us. We feel we must strive to overcome it.

2 Human reason suggests that the way to deal with the gulf is to keep the commandments. So ***we set out to jump the gulf***; namely, to keep the commandments to achieve our goal. However, in doing this, we put the commandments to a use God never intended.

3 We feel so ***smug***, so ***self-satisfied***. After all, we made it across 3½ of the commandments. We feel saintly about *the good we have done*.

4 However, there is a serious question we must ask ourselves: "What are we going to do about *the good we have left undone—about the 6½ commandments we have not kept?*" Sin is not merely *doing wrong* (sins of *commission*); it is also *failing to do right* (sins of *omission*).

In James 2:10, James writes:

> *Whoever keeps the whole law but fails in one point has become accountable for all of it.*

In Romans 3:19,20, Paul writes:

> *Now we know that whatever the law says, it speaks to those who are under the law, so that every mouth may be silenced, and the whole world be held accountable to God. For "no human being will be justified in his sight" by deeds prescribed by the law, for through the law comes the knowledge of sin.*

The Cross Is the Crossing

In Romans 3:23, Paul writes, "All have sinned and fall short of the glory of God." **ILLUSTRATION 22E** uses this passage to further develop **ILLUSTRATION 22D**. The numbers below refer to the four sections of **ILLUSTRATION 22E**.

 People become aware of the gulf sin has made between themselves and God.

 They dress themselves in their most virtuous clothes ("good deeds")—complete with ***angelic wings*** and "holy hat" (***halo***). In doing this, they hope to bring themselves into fellowship with God.

 All human attempts to overcome the gulf between God and themselves fail. They are the product of misguided, human *do-it-yourself* religions. Our self-made angelic wings and holy hat are of no value in the salvation process. God never intended God's commandments to be used this way.

 God has provided the bridge. God offers free and full forgiveness to humanity on the basis of the saving life, death, and resurrection of Jesus the Messiah. We are not saved by a thing of wood (***cross***), but by the Person who died on it (***crowned Jesus***). The process is:

> ❶ Jesus comes to us, gathers us into His arms, and
>
> ❷ takes us ***across*** the ***crossing*** via the ***cross*** into God's presence.

How Many Religions?

Many believe that although there are hundreds of religions in the world, they all teach much the same thing: "Believe in God and try to be good. If you do that, you'll make it into heaven!"

ILLUSTRATION 22F shows the *only two things* that people can and do trust in for salvation. One is a *human delusion*—salvation by works. The other is *divine truth*—God's gracious, saving action in Jesus the Messiah.

Upper section

Let's call the ship in the upper center of the illustration *The Good Ship God* (**ship with symbol for God on its side**), and let's think of humanity as having fallen overboard into *The Ocean of Sin and Death* (**waves with symbols for sin and death on them**). We are in danger! We shall drown unless rescued!

What are we to cling to? There are two possibilities:

◆ *The life preserver of good works*, the supposed good deeds we offer to God (**arrow rising up to God**, **law-codes**, *left*).

◆ *The life preserver of Jesus the Messiah and His saving work* (**arrow descending from God**, **crowned crucified Jesus; rope linking the life preserver to "The Good Ship God"**, *right*) Note that only this preserver is linked to God!)

The life preserver of good works is a delusion. It never has saved. It never will save. It cannot save. Yet many people cling to it, for they believe their supposed good life will move God to accept them. **Salvation is found only in what God makes available to fallen humanity: Jesus the Messiah—sinless, crucified, risen, and reigning.**

The illustration has certain limitations. God does not merely throw out saving equipment from the cozy comfort of God's "captain's cabin." In Jesus, God plunged into our midst, into the midst of humanity, to rescue us from eternal death. God persuades and empowers us to move our hands from the life preserver of *works* to the life preserver of *salvation in Jesus*.

Sometimes those whom God lovingly hauls aboard *The Good Ship God* plunge overboard once more, and God must go to their rescue again—and sometimes again and again.

Furthermore, sometimes those whom God hauls aboard *The Good Ship God* busy themselves with concerns about the ship's menu, air-conditioning system, recreation program, and comfort level—but fail to search for others still overboard and in danger. They become *keepers of the aquarium* rather than *fishers of people, rescuers of the lost*. They show little interest in drawing others aboard.

Lower section

Humanity stands either *under law* (**person under law-codes**), or *under a gracious God* (**person under symbol for God**) for salvation. It is either-or; it is never both-and.

Note that neither person has hands raised in praise. God does not choose those willing to be saved, for none are willing. In the final analysis, God—patiently and graciously—makes the unwilling willing.

1. KNOW
2. ASSENT
3. TRUST

Saving Faith

The Nature of Saving Faith

Some use the term *faith* vaguely. They say "one must have faith," but do not specify in whom or in what that faith must be. They usually mean that one must believe that "things will work out all right in the end."

ILLUSTRATION 22G builds on **ILLUSTRATION 22E** to define what the Bible means by saving faith. Saving faith consists of the following:

KNOW

Believers know who Jesus is, why Jesus' saving work was necessary, and what Jesus did for fallen humanity, 2 Timothy 1:12.

ASSENT

Believers agree that they are reconciled to God and have fellowship with Him only through what Jesus did for them, Acts 16:31.

TRUST

Believers trust in Jesus' saving life, death, and resurrection for salvation, Romans 8:38,39.

The Function of Saving Faith

Why does faith save?

- Faith does not save by virtue of its *action*, as though faith is some "special deed."
- Faith saves by virtue of its *object* (what it clings to), the person and saving work of Jesus the Messiah. **ILLUSTRATION 22G** shows people clinging, not to *something within* themselves, but to *Someone outside* themselves (***Servant-King***, ***cross***, ***tomb***, ***rising arrow*** symbolizing Jesus' resurrection and ascension).

Saving faith, then, is not a good work that we do; it is *God's gracious gift* to us, and *God's gracious creation* within us. Jesus saves, and saving faith clings to Jesus. God is not lost—and we do not find God. We are lost—and God finds us, Luke 15.

There is no such thing as private Christianity. *Personal* faith, yes. *Private* faith, no! Hence, **ILLUSTRATION 22G** shows two pairs of hands clinging to a life preserver. To belong to Jesus is to belong to Jesus' *community*, to care for its members on a world-wide basis, and to seek to draw others into that community.

By GRACE!
Through FAITH!
For SERVICE!

Degrees—of What?

Of Being Saved? No!

 ILLUSTRATION 22H depicts the attitude some people (***person at bottom step***) have toward professional church workers and clergy (***person at top step***). They think, "My faith is so weak! I wish I had a faith as strong as theirs. Then I would feel closer to God and more sure of being saved." They think that the stronger the faith, the greater the possibility of being saved. They almost think of their faith, their act of believing, as something that earns them forgiveness.

 However, establishing fellowship with God is not something brought about by people. We do not establish fellowship with God by striving to climb ever higher on the "intensity of faith ***staircase***." People are not saved by developing within themselves a required level of faith. Salvation is always a matter of trust in God's free, forgiving, and saving *grace*.

 The ground at the foot of the cross is level (***two persons kneeling—on level ground—either side of the crowned, crucified Jesus the Messiah***). "There is no difference," Romans 3:23. All Christians need, and cling to, the same Jesus the Messiah. Jesus saves; faith clings to Jesus.

Of Response to Jesus? Yes!

Although people show different *degrees of fervor* in clinging to, and following, Jesus the Messiah, no Christian is more saved than another.

 God wants people to grow in grace and in the knowledge of the Lord Jesus Christ, 2 Peter 3:18. This growth is a *response* to salvation, not a *reason* for it.

 God's gracious will is that we use whatever abilities God provides to His glory in the service of others, Mark 12:28–31. Some have been endowed with more ability than others, Matthew 25:14–30. Some have more opportunity to serve than others, Matthew 20:1–16. God wants each person to glorify God by serving others, according to the measure of ability and opportunity God provides.

 Even if we did everything God asks us to do (which we cannot!), we would still have to confess that we are unworthy servants who have done nothing beyond the call of duty, Luke 17:10.

 The prepositions Paul uses in Ephesians 2:8–10 are significant. He says that we are saved **by GRACE**, **through FAITH**, **for SERVICE**.

- ◆ **GRACE** is the basis of salvation.

- ◆ **FAITH** is the hand that lays hold of grace.

- ◆ **SERVICE** of others (and so, God) is the response to receiving and taking hold of grace through faith.

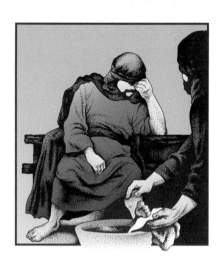

22A Since the fall into sin, people look to either human works or divine forgiveness to be made right with God. The first is a human delusion; only trust in God's forgiveness through Jesus the Messiah can make us right with God.

22B The Bible uses a number of words to describe human nature before God. Sin is basically human nature in revolt against God. This sinful *condition* produces sinful *deeds*.

22C Sin manifests itself in numerous ways. Many people do not understand that one can be *respectable in the eyes of society*, but *useless before God*.

22D People are quick to boast of the *little good* they have *done*, but slow to acknowledge the *much good* they have left *undone*.

22E All human efforts to overcome the gulf between God and self lead only to death and destruction. These efforts put the commandments to a use God never intended. Only Jesus' saving work can overcome the gulf between God and humanity.

22F All people cling either to their own so-called *good works*, or to *God's grace* in Jesus the Messiah. Only the latter can save.

22G Faith does not save by virtue of *what it does*. It saves by virtue of *what it clings to*—the completed, saving work of Jesus the Messiah.

22H Although some people trust in and respond to Jesus with greater fervor than others, all who trust in Jesus for salvation are *equally saved*.

THE DIVINE DRAMA®

OUR NARRATIVE

UNIT 23

When the End Comes

What the Bible teaches about the end of time and life after death ("the Last Things") is often the final chapter in books on Christian teaching. This manual studies it in Unit 23 rather than Unit 30 to stress that Christians possess eternal life *already in this life*. Although Christians are not *in* heaven, they *possess* heaven. **ILLUSTRATION 23A**, **ILLUSTRATION 23B**, and **ILLUSTRATION 23C** will build on one another to present this grand truth, and to point out how citizens of God's eternal kingdom are to live in this present life.

ILLUSTRATION 23A compares what the Pharisees and Sadducees taught about life after death with what Jesus teaches about it.

Upper section

Some in ancient Israel looked on death as a grim affair (**tombstone with skull**). They begged God not to let them die, for they feared that after death they would be cut off from God forever, Psalm 88:1–12.

The *Pharisees* taught that the dead would be raised on the Last Day of this present age to face **JUDGMENT**. Those who lived a righteous life would experience **RESURRECTION** to participate in the Messianic Age that would take place in the land of Israel, Isaiah 25:8, 26:19; Daniel 12:1–3. How long the Messianic Age would last was debated. Some thought that it would last for a thousand years, and then it would be over. **ETERNAL LIFE** was not a consideration.

The *Sadducees* did not believe in the resurrection of the body. They taught that those who died continued to live on in a shadowy form (as "shades") in Sheol, the realm of the dead. The dead were cut off from God and forgotten by God, Psalm 6:5. The Sadducees confronted Jesus with a story designed to ridicule what He taught about the resurrection of the body and life after death, Mark 12:18–27.

Lower section

Jesus, the final interpreter of all Scripture, transcended and transformed the teachings of the Pharisees and Sadducees. Jesus speaks the *final word* about **JUDGMENT**, **RESURRECTION**, and **ETERNAL LIFE**, for Jesus' Father has given Him all authority to determine the nature and outcome of these issues, John 5:22–29.

◆ People are judged already in this life on the basis of what they do with Jesus' offer of forgiveness and call to discipleship. Those who, in faith, embrace Jesus as Savior and Lord possess eternal life already in this life, John 5:24,39,40; 10:27,28; 11:25,26; 17:2,3. This life and the next life overlap, for, in Jesus, the *eternal realm* has already broken into this *present realm*.

◆ Hebrews 9:27,28 teaches that when Jesus reappears at the end of time, He will not do so to deal with human sin. Jesus has already dealt with that. On the Last Day, Jesus, when gathering all people and nations before Him, will make a public declaration of the relationship to Him that existed already in this life, John 5:28,29; 8:24; Matthew 25:31–34; Romans 8:1.

◆ In Matthew 25:34, Jesus tells what He will say to His own when He greets them on that Last Day: "Come, you that are blessed by my Father, inherit the kingdom prepared for you from the foundation of the world." **The grand truth is that Jesus will welcome into His eternal home those who have believed in, trusted, and followed Him (*glorified Jesus with arms extended in welcome*).**

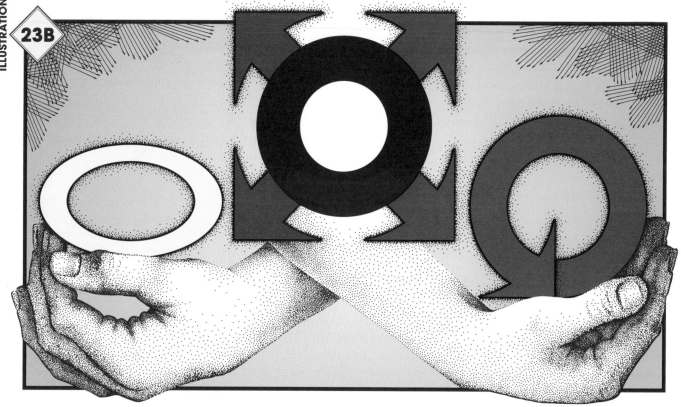

Upper section

The upper section of **ILLUSTRATION 23B** shows the *symbol for God*, with *arms extended from it*. The arms are *crossed over*. In the one to the *left* is a *halo*. In the one to the *right* is the *symbol for sin*. What is the message?

In 2 Corinthians 5:21, Paul speaks of the *great exchange*, the *sweet swap*, that God brought about through Jesus' life, death, and resurrection. Paul says that God took all our sins and put them on Jesus. Furthermore, God takes all Jesus' achievements and gives them to us. Hence, Jesus' holiness (*halo*) is given to us, and our sin (*symbol for sin*) is given to Jesus. Jesus took humanity's sin to the cross, and suffered what it deserves. Jesus won forgiveness *for* the world, and offers that forgiveness *to* the world.

Lower section

For Christians, the outcome of history's Last Day is not in doubt. The decisions relating to them have already been made—by Jesus!

◆ Jesus says that when finally He returns in glory, He will command all graves to give up their dead, and gather all nations before Him, John 5:28,29; 1 Corinthians 15:12–28; Matthew 25:31. Jesus will separate humanity into two groups, the *sheep* and the *goats*, Matthew 25:32,33. Jesus will *welcome the sheep* (*glorified Jesus with arms extended in welcome*) and invite them to enter the Eternal Home He has prepared for them. However, Jesus will *reject the goats*.

◆ What will influence the *welcome* and the *rejection*? In Ephesians 2:8–10, Paul points out that we, God's people, are saved *by grace, through faith, for service*. **Although we are never saved *by* service, we are always saved *for* service.** Although on that Last Day, Jesus will *welcome* us into His Eternal Home on the basis of His forgiving grace (the basis of *acceptance*), Jesus will also *commend* us on the basis of service we have rendered to others (the basis of *commendation*).

◆ In welcoming the *sheep*, Jesus points out something surprising—but of great importance for God's people. If we ask *people*, "How many people live on Planet Earth?" they say, "About six billion." If we ask *Jesus* the same question, He replies, "Two—you and Me! To you, everyone else is Me—in disguise." In Matthew 25:40, Jesus says to those whom He welcomes:

  Truly, I tell you, just as you did it to one of the least of those who are members of my family, you did it to Me.

◆ Jesus links Himself "in disguise" to those who are hungry, thirsty, lonely, lacking clothes, sick, and in prison. Those whom Jesus welcomes and commends express surprise. When they served as they did, they did not do it for the sake of merit or notice, Matthew 25:37–39. *They did it out of compassion.*

◆ Those whom Jesus rejects and condemns to eternal separation are not rebuked for harm they did to anyone. The point is this: Although they *address* Jesus as "Lord," they are rejected for having failed to *follow* Jesus as Lord—for having failed to devote life to glorifying Jesus by living to serve others, Matthew 25:41–46. They lived to satisfy their own whims and desires.

ILLUSTRATION 23C will develop the implications of Jesus' teachings in relation to these matters.

23C

The Welcome Home God's people will receive on that Last Day is made possible only by the goodness and forgiving mercy of God. Jesus welcomes His own with, "Come, you that are *blessed by My Father.*" *Jesus' Father alone* is responsible for their being blessed. Jesus invites them to *inherit* the Kingdom; *inherit* implies a *gift.* The Kingdom was prepared *for* them, not *by* them. *Merit plays no role.*

ILLUSTRATION 23C consists of three parts.
The message of the *upper section* has been explained in **ILLUSTRATION 23B**.

Middle section

◆ Jesus will graciously commend those He welcomes for acts of service done to others (*servant figures*). For example, they gave **food** to the hungry, **drink** to the thirsty, **companionship to the lonely**, and **clothing** to those lacking it. They also visited and cared for the sick (*symbol of healing,* **serpent around staff**; see Numbers 21:4–9), and visited the **prisoner**. In serving people in these situations of need, they were really serving Jesus "in distressing disguise"—a term used by Mother Theresa, a Catholic nun, whose faith in Jesus inspired her to devote life to caring for the desperately poor and needy.

◆ Jesus will reject those who claimed to know Him as their "Lord" (Matthew 25:44), but never followed Jesus in servant discipleship. Jesus does not refer to any evil that they might have done, but to the good they failed to do. They failed to see Jesus all around them in distressing disguise.

Lower section

◆ *Food and drink* (*left*): The Gospels frequently refer to Jesus sharing a meal with His disciples and followers. Jesus' followers today need to understand that Jesus is present with them constantly (Matthew 28:20), and in a very meaningful way at every mealtime. In Jesus' day, those who ate together declared: "We are family! We will serve each other, and defend each other to the death!"

◆ *Basin and towel* (*right*): Jesus' followers are to serve each other, even as Jesus served His disciples by washing their feet.

◆ *Drop of water—Baptism* (*center*): When people are baptized, they are adopted into God's family and God shares Jesus' sinless life, death, burial, and resurrection with them, Romans 6:1–14. Jesus says to those adopted into His Kingdom in Baptism: "I lived the life you were meant to live—but have not lived and cannot live. I give you My sinless life to possess as your very own. You can look on My life as though you yourself lived it. You went to the cross with Me—and because I shared My cross with you, you no longer need to suffer any punishment for sin. You went into the tomb with Me, and so have already endured the grave that sin brings. I rose from the dead, and I share My resurrection with you. Eternal life is already yours. You merely wait to join Me in that eternal realm you already possess. So while you wait to join Me in heaven, *seek to live the heavenly life already on earth.*"

◆ *Bread and cup* (*center*): Jesus' spiritual brothers and sisters are "re-membered" to Him in the Holy Communion—that is, linked to Jesus and His saving work, and to each other. Having celebrated their membership in Jesus' community by eating what they are (i.e., the body of Christ), they go forth to become what they eat. They seek to make Jesus visible in all they do by living as Jesus' servant-people in community.

23D

After the Last Heartbeat, What Then?

Christians know that the life to come is in good hands—God's hands. However, being human, they are curious about what people experience after death. The Bible says something about this.

 Some early Christians in Thessalonica were confused about Jesus' reappearing. They feared that those who died prior to Jesus' reappearing would miss out on the Eternal Age Jesus would establish. Paul reminded them that when Jesus reappears, He will raise the dead to participate in the life to come, 1 Thessalonians 4:13–18.

> *For since we believe that Jesus died and rose again, even so through Jesus, God will bring with Him those who have fallen asleep.* (4:14, RSV translation)

Note Paul's terms. Jesus *died*. His own *fall asleep*. The term *fall asleep* denotes that death is not the end. Jesus will wake us from our "death sleep," Mark 5:39; Luke 7:14,15; John 11:43,44.

 The Bible says a limited amount about the condition of those who fall asleep in Jesus. Paul is content to speak of life after death as being "with Christ," which he insists is "far better," Philippians 1:23. Paul also tells us that when Jesus finally raises our bodies from the dead, our resurrected "spiritual" body will be *similar* to our present body, but *adapted* for eternal life in an eternal world, 1 Corinthians 15:35–58.

With Angels and Archangels

The Revelation to John offers a number of glimpses of life in God's presence. Its visions contain *impressions of the glory* of heaven, rather than *details of the dimensions* of heaven. **ILLUSTRATION 23D** draws on Revelation chs. 4 and 5 to depict the wonder of God's eternal presence.

 God is on His ***heavenly throne***. Splendor abounds. Around God is a circle of 24 thrones. On each sits an elder (a church leader), clothed in white, and wearing a *golden crown* (***24 crowns***). Some suggest the number "24" refers to "Old Israel" (12 tribes) and New Israel (12 apostles). At the four corners of the throne's platform are four heavenly creatures. Each depicts one of God's qualities. The ***lion***, the king of the wild beasts, depicts *awesomeness;* the ***ox***, the king of the domestic beasts, depicts *strength;* the ***man***, *wisdom;* the ***eagle***, *mobility*. Each creature is covered with ***eyes***, signifying God's *unceasing watchfulness*. The beasts and elders sing God's praises, 4:8b,11.

 The triumphant Jesus, the ***Lamb*** that was slain (***cross***), is alive and stands next to His Father's throne, 5:6. In His hands Jesus holds ***a scroll sealed with seven seals***. The message is: Jesus has authority over creation and holds the keys to human history, 5:6,7.

 Beyond the circle of 24 elders is another circle of thousands of angels, 5:11 (***wings***). They too sing their song of praise. Beyond them is yet another circle of "every creature in heaven and on earth and under the earth and in the sea" (***circle of male and female figures, praising God***). They, too, sing their own song, 5:13b.

 Those already in God's presence take part in a heavenly banquet, Revelation 19:9. God's people on earth take part in the same banquet (***bread and cup***, *lower left corner*) while waiting to join the host in God's heavenly realm. (Units 24 and 25 deal with this heavenly banquet.)

Whether we live or die, we are in good hands—God's hands!

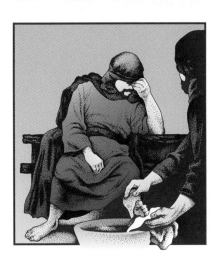

23A Jesus clarified ideas about death and eternity that prevailed prior to and during His ministry. Jesus teaches that those who belong to Him in faith and love have passed from death to life, already possess heaven, and merely wait to enter what they already possess.

23B Christians can be sure about the reception they will receive on that Last Day when God will gather all humanity before Him. Christians know that:

- God has taken all their sin and placed it on His Son, Jesus the Messiah.
- God has taken all that His Son, Jesus the Messiah, achieved for sinful humanity and given it to people to be received in faith.

At the same time, those who believe and trust in what Jesus the Messiah did for them know that while they wait for that final "Welcome Home" into heaven, they are to seek constantly to walk through life following and reflecting their Lord and Savior, Jesus the Messiah, Jesus *the Good Shepherd*. They are to live as "joyous sheep," not as "stubborn goats" who live only for themselves.

23C Jesus assures us that when He returns on the last day of history, Jesus will welcome His family, His "sheep," into the Eternal Home He has already prepared for them. Jesus will also reject those whom He will address as "goats"—those who claimed to know Jesus as Savior but made no effort to follow Him as Lord.

23D The Bible provides us with glimpses of the nature of life in heaven. It assures us that Jesus will one day wake us from death to live eternally in His presence.

THE DIVINE DRAMA®

OUR NARRATIVE

UNIT 24

With Angels and Archangels
(The Lord's Supper)

ILLUSTRATION
24A

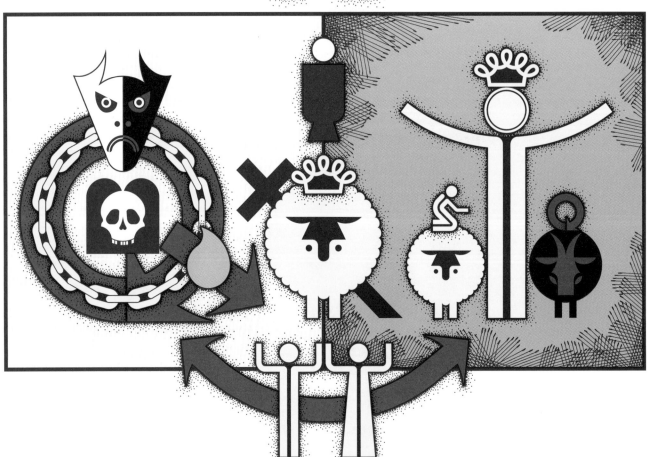

Upper section

The upper section of **ILLUSTRATION 24A** depicts how the Israelites understood their annual celebration of the festival of Passover. During the celebration, the people shared a meal at which they ate a **lamb** (*center*) and several other foods, including unleavened bread, Exodus 12:33,34. The meal reminded the Israelites how God had *passed over their homes* but had *passed through the homes of the Egyptians* (killing the firstborn of the Egyptian children and cattle, Exodus 12:29), and how *God had finally led the Israelites out of Egypt*, Exodus 13:17–14:31 (*left section*).

The Passover meal looked two ways (***double-headed arrow pointing backward and forward***). It looked *backward* to the first great rescue event, the Exodus from Egypt. It looked *forward* to the time when the long expected Messiah (***star of David***), the king of the Jews (***crown***), would come to rescue God's people from their political enemies and usher in the Messianic Age.

Lower section

In Jesus, God's Messianic King (***crown***) finally came. Jesus is the Lamb of God (***lamb***) who takes away the sin of the world through His death on the cross, John 1:29,36; see also 1 Corinthians 5:7,8.

Jesus rescued humanity from bondage (***chains***)

◆ to the powers of sin (***symbol for sin***),

◆ the demonic (***satanic face***),

◆ laws and rules (***law-codes***), and

◆ death (***skull***).

Through Holy Baptism, we share in Jesus' saving work (***drop of water on the arrow that passes through chains***). Through Holy Baptism, Jesus leads us from bondage to hostile powers into the only true freedom—membership in Jesus' community. In that community, we look to Jesus for guidance and inspiration so that we might no longer walk through life as stubborn goats, living only to serve self (***goat, symbol for sin*** to *Jesus' left*), but rather follow our Good Shepherd King as grateful, obedient sheep, seeking to serve God and others in all we do—even as Jesus did (***sheep, servant figure*** to *Jesus' right*).

When we partake of the Lord's Supper (***bread and cup***), we celebrate ("re-member") the fact that we share in Jesus' victory over our foes. We look two ways (***double-headed arrow pointing backward and forward***): *backward* to our rescue from Satan, sin, law, and death, and *forward* to Jesus' reappearing, 1 Corinthians 11:26.

On the Last Day of history, when Jesus reappears and brings history to an end, He will separate the **sheep** from the **goats** (Matthew 25:31–46), and welcome His sheep into His eternal home (***glorified Jesus with arms extended in welcome***, *right*). There, what Revelation 19:9 refers to as "the marriage supper of the Lamb" will continue to all eternity.

24B

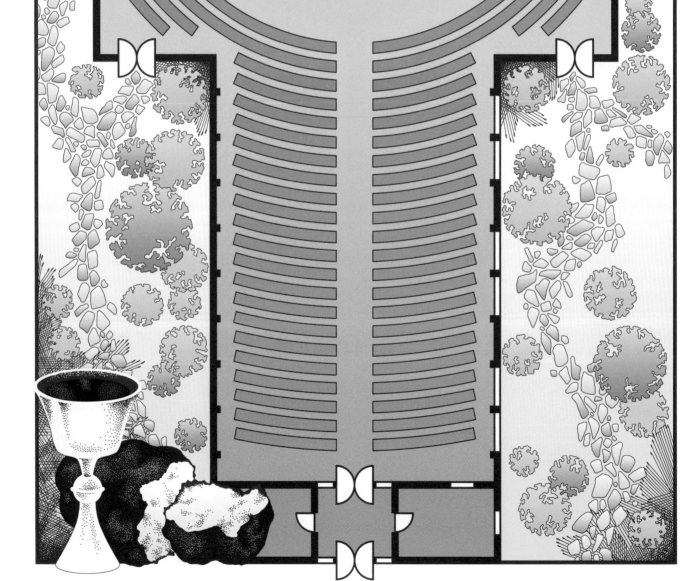

 People build churches in various styles. Some design them to reflect their beliefs, or to harmonize with the surrounding landscape. Centuries ago, those who built cathedrals and churches sought to create within them the atmosphere of heaven itself—a setting in which people might experience a sense of God's presence.

 ILLUSTRATION 24B depicts a church in the form of a cross—still the ground plan for many churches today. The two crossing sections are called the *transept* and *nave*. The term nave is derived from the Latin word for "ship." It suggests that the church is the vessel that takes God's people across the oceans of this world into the eternal harbor of heaven.

 In many churches, when worship begins, the worship leaders walk in procession towards the altar during the *Introit* (a Latin word meaning *he enters*).

 Ancient churches contained two *ambos*, or lecterns, holding Bibles. Two Old Testament readings and a section of a New Testament epistle (letter) were read from **the lectern to the right** (as viewed facing the altar), and a portion of a Gospel was read from **the lectern to the left**.

 The illustration depicts an **altar-in-the-round**, as seen in some of today's churches—which themselves sometimes have a round ground plan. The layout reminds worshipers that the risen Lord (**glorified**—but present—**Jesus**) lives in the midst of His community, whose members are to serve one another.

 The **broken loaf and chalice** (*lower left*) depict the bread and wine used in the Lord's Supper. In this meal, the worshiping community shares *on earth* the meal it will eventually celebrate eternally *in heaven*.

The Old Testament Hope

 In Isaiah 25:6, the prophet describes what ancient Israel believed God would do for His people when the Messianic Age arrived:

> On this mountain the Lord of hosts will make for all peoples a feast of rich food, a feast of well-aged wines, of rich food filled with marrow, of well-aged wines strained clear.

 The image of God dining with God's people is used numerous times in the Old Testament to describe the joys of the coming Messianic Age, Psalm 23:5; Isaiah 55:1f; 65:11–13.

The New Testament Fulfillment

 When Jesus ate with people, Jesus was doing more than sharing a meal to satisfy hunger. Jesus was inviting the participants to share in the Messianic Banquet, Mark 2:15,16; 6:30–44; 8:1-10; Luke 7:33,34; 13:29; 22:30; 24:30; Revelation 3:20.

 Prior to His ascension, Jesus assured the disciples that He would remain with them until His final appearing, Matthew 28:20. Jesus has not *withdrawn* His physical presence; He has *transformed* it. **Jesus will remain among the members of His community, invisibly, until the end of this present age.** The entry point into God's community is *Holy Baptism* (**arrow**, **drop of water**, *lower center*)—in which God adopts people into His family and makes them participants in, sharers in, all that Jesus the Messiah was, is, and achieved for them.

 Revelation 19:9 states that in heaven God's people will share "the marriage supper of the Lamb." However, God's people begin to partake of that marriage supper already on earth, in that they celebrate their membership in God's eternal family in a special way in the meal variously called: the Lord's Supper, Holy Communion, the Eucharist, the Lord's Table, the Mass (**bread and cup**).

 Some of the worship forms Christians use to celebrate this special meal declare, "Therefore with angels and archangels, and with all the company of heaven …" (see Revelation chs. 4,5 and **ILLUSTRATION 23D**).

 ILLUSTRATION 24C depicts *an altar plan that is circular*. The *glorified Jesus* in our midst shares Himself with us through His Holy Meal. Jesus' will is that we who participate in this meal serve those within our church family, and within the world community, as He has served us.

This section serves as an appendix to Units 23 and 24. Its goal is to explain the worship rituals some churches have used for centuries—and still use today.

Worship patterns differ among and within denominations. Some are highly structured; others are simple. Some are conducted with great dignity; others are casual in tone.

Some churches use liturgies based on ancient practices. To understand their meaning, let's attend a worship service that might have been held somewhere in Europe a thousand years ago. (We will imagine that a guide is explaining explain what is happening.)

We shall observe the three major sections in the service:

◆ **THE CONFESSION OF SINS AND ABSOLUTION**

◆ **THE LITURGY OF THE WORD**

◆ **THE LITURGY OF THE UPPER ROOM**

THE CONFESSION OF SINS AND ABSOLUTION

Our guide explains: When we come into this house of worship, we come into the presence of the Triune God. The priest acknowledges that by saying, "In the name of the Father, the Son, and the Holy Spirit." (*Invocation*)

We know that we have no right to come to God through our own merits. We are sinners. Our sin has built a wall between God and us; we can do nothing about removing it. The people confess their sins to acknowledge this. (*Confession*)

Hear what the worship leader is saying. He is telling the people that God has forgiven them for Christ's sake. The words he speaks on God's behalf are very meaningful to us. "Your sins are forgiven. His peace be with you…that your joy may be full." (*Absolution*)

THE LITURGY OF THE WORD

The people are waiting for the worship to begin. See! The clergy are ready to enter. They begin to walk down the aisle toward the altar, the symbol of God's presence. The clergy symbolize the whole congregation drawing near to God. The people and choir are singing verses from a Psalm. The clergy approach the altar with joy and confidence. Because of what Jesus has done for us, we may come to God with boldness. (*Introit;* Latin, "he enters." See Hebrews 4:16.)

The clergy have now come to the altar. Everyone is singing, "Glory be to the Father, and to the Son, and to the Holy Spirit…" (*Gloria Patri;* Latin, "Glory to the Father")

We, God's people, are now in God's presence. God has told us to come with boldness and confidence before His throne of grace, and we have come! Now we ask God to bestow His good gifts on us. Hear the words: "Lord, have mercy!" (*Kyrie;* Greek, "O Lord." See Hebrews 4:16.)

We are assured of God's kindness and mercy. That's why everybody sings words used by the angels on the night Jesus was born, "Glory to God in the highest." If God gave us His own Son, God will give us those gracious gifts that equip us to praise and serve Him. (*Gloria in Excelsis;* Luke 2:1–20)

The priest is greeting the people, "The Lord be with you." The people respond by asking that the Lord might be with him also. (*Salutation*)

The priest now leads the people in a prayer based on the central message of today's readings and service. There was a time when the local priest met with his people every day at the door of the local church to offer prayers about the community's needs. He "collected" them—which is why the present prayer is called the *Collect*.

Now that the prayer has been offered, a deacon is moving towards the lectern to the right of the altar to read three Bible passages. He will read two passages from the Old Testament, and one from a New Testament letter. (*Scripture Readings*)

The deacon has completed the readings and is moving back to his seat. Another deacon is moving towards the lectern on the left side of the altar to read the Gospel. The people sing while the deacons take these steps. (*Gradual;* Latin, "gradus" means "step.")

The reading of the Gospel is a high point for us. Jesus speaks to us through it. A candle-bearer stands on each side of the deacon as he reads to remind us of Jesus, the Light of the world. All the people stand to listen. If a king is present, he takes off his crown; he knows he is in the presence of the King of kings. Soldiers who are present unbuckle their swords and place them on the floor. (*The Gospel*)

Now that Jesus has spoken to us through His Word, we all join in confessing our faith in Father, Son, and Holy Spirit. We are confessing a truth, not offering a prayer. (*Creed;* Latin "credo," I believe)

The presbyter is preparing to explain the message of today's Bible readings, and their meaning for our lives today. The presbyter sometimes sits behind the altar while he speaks to the people. Today many speak from a pulpit. (*The Sermon*)

Note how the presbyter greets the people before the sermon. He uses a greeting written by one of the apostles. After his sermon, he will speak a word of peace to the people, assuring them that God has thoughts of kindness and peace toward us. (*Votum*)

The people now offer gifts for use in God's Kingdom. Centuries ago they used to bring tokens and samples of their daily labor and handiwork—perhaps grain, bread, and cloth. These things were distributed among the needy. Today we bring money. God has told us how He has given Himself for us, and we offer God tokens of our own lives in response. (*The Offering*)

More detailed prayers are now being offered. We praise God for who God is and what He does for us. We pray for our leaders in all walks of life. We pray for the Church around the world and for our Church here. We pray for our needs. We pray for the sick. We ask God to help us be more like Jesus. We pray to be kept close to Jesus throughout this life, and look forward to being with Jesus in heaven when this life is over. (*The Prayers*)

Hear how the whole congregation joins in praying the prayer Jesus gave to God's people. We wish to have our lives reflect Jesus' life more and more. (*The Lord's Prayer*)

THE LITURGY OF THE UPPER ROOM

The clergy are now getting ready for the final part of the service. This will be the high point of our celebration. They are preparing the bread and wine to celebrate the Holy Meal Jesus gave to the disciples in the upper room the night before He was put to death.

The liturgist is singing: "…therefore with angels and archangels, and with all the company of heaven…" Although we still live on earth, we are members of God's heavenly community and are about to share the heavenly meal (see Rev. 4,5; 19:9).

Hear the words, "Holy, holy, holy." Those who live in God's presence in heaven sing that song (see Isaiah 6:3; Rev. 4:8). We join in with them because we are already members of the heavenly company. (*Sanctus*)

The presbyter is repeating the words Jesus used in the upper room, "This is my body. This is my blood of the covenant, which is poured out for many." (*The Words of Institution*)

The people are singing their praises to the living Jesus, the Lamb of God who was slain for our sins, but is alive now and forever, and about to give us His most precious gift—Himself! (*Agnus Dei;* Latin, "Lamb of God")

Members of the congregation are receiving the Holy Meal. This is a moment of joy for us all! Jesus has come to us and given Himself to us. We have seen God's salvation, and go on our way in peace. We are so blessed! We are not to hoard Jesus for ourselves; we are to share Him with all people. Jesus is God's light for humanity. (*Nunc Dimittis;* Latin, "Now send us on our way"; Luke 2:29–32)

Before we depart, we offer a final prayer to thank God for His undeserved kindness. We ask God to increase our faith in His continuing presence among us, and our trust in God's care. We ask God to empower us to live and serve all people as He has loved and served us. (*The Thanksgiving*)

Our worship is almost over! God, through the priest, speaks a parting blessing as we leave. God assures us He will bless and keep us in all we do, and look on us at all times with a smile on His face. We go forth in peace to serve God wherever we are, in whatever we do. (*The Benediction*)

POINTS TO PONDER

24A When Old Testament believers worshiped, they looked two ways—backward and forward. They looked *backward* to the Exodus-Sinai events, and *forward* to the time when God would rescue them in the Messianic Age.

New Testament believers similarly look backward and forward in worship—*backward* to the saving events of Jesus' life, death, and resurrection, and *forward* to their final deliverance on the Last Day.

24B Down through the centuries, Christians have erected buildings to help and inspire them in their worship of God. Some of these buildings were designed to suggest the atmosphere of heaven itself, others to reflect the presence of the Risen Christ in the midst of His worshiping, serving community.

24C The heart of Christian worship is the conviction that the victorious Jesus is in our midst—to assure us of His forgiveness, and to inspire us to love and serve one another as Jesus continues to love and serve us.

THE DIVINE DRAMA.

OUR NARRATIVE

UNIT 25
Preparing for the Banquet

25A

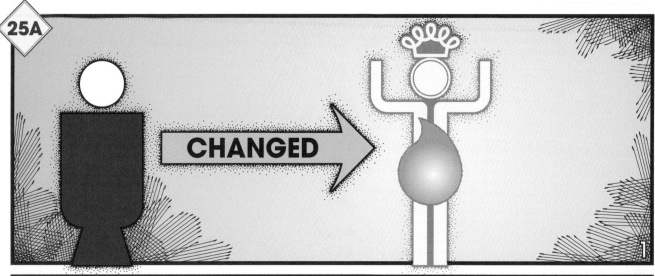

CHANGED

REPRESENTS

GOD ADDS +

The first three Gospels tell of Jesus introducing His Holy Supper, Matthew 26:26–29; Mark 14:22–24; Luke 22:14–20.

In Mark 14:22–24, we read:

> *While they were eating* [the Passover], *Jesus took a loaf of bread, and after blessing it He broke it, and gave it to them, and said, "Take; this is my body." Then He took a cup, and after giving thanks He gave it to them, and all of them drank from it. He said to them, "This is my blood of the new covenant, which is poured out for many."*

In 1 Corinthians 10:16, Paul writes in relation to the Lord's Supper:

> *The cup of blessing that we bless, is it not a sharing in the blood of Christ? The bread that we break, is it not a sharing in the body of Christ?*

ILLUSTRATION 25A depicts the three main views within the Christian family around the world concerning what worshipers eat and drink when participating in the Lord's Supper:

The Bread and Wine Are CHANGED into Jesus' Body and Blood

Some teach that during the worship service, God empowers the officiating priest or pastor to *change* bread and wine into the body and blood of Jesus the Messiah. Although what the worshipers eat and drink have all the outward appearances of bread and wine, it is no longer bread and wine, but the body and blood of Jesus.

Two things, bread and wine, are changed into *two different things*—the body and blood of Christ.

The Bread and Wine REPRESENT Jesus' Body and Blood

Some teach that the bread and wine (sometimes grape juice) are symbols and reminders of Jesus' body and blood. The bread *represents* Jesus' body, and the wine *represents* Jesus' blood.

Two things, bread and wine, remain *two things*—bread and wine.

Together with the Bread and Wine, GOD ADDS Jesus' Body and Blood

Some teach that, although the bread remains bread and the wine remains wine, Jesus gives us His true body together with the bread and His true blood together with the wine. They do not teach that one could find a *visible* part of Jesus' body within the bread, or a *visible* drop of Jesus' blood within the wine. They speak of this *true presence* as sacramental and spiritual—real, but a mystery.

Although the bread and the wine remain bread and wine, they become the bearers of *two additional things*—the sacramental, spiritual-but-real, body and blood of Jesus. The worshiper receives *four things*.

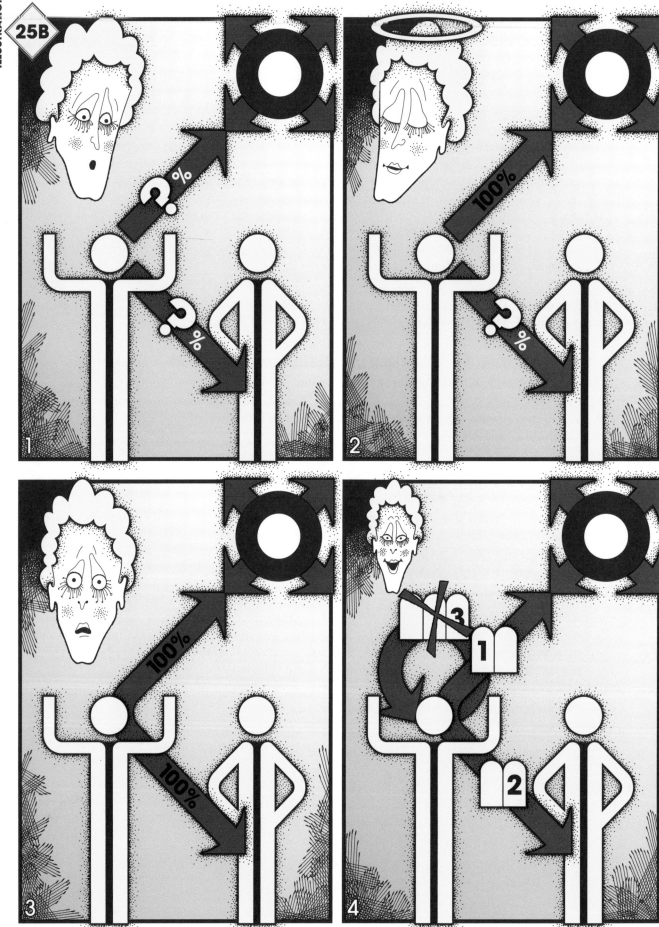

Jesus the Messiah welded the two key Old Testament commandments (Deuteronomy 6:4,5 and Leviticus 19:18) into a *single commandment*—but a single commandment with *two arms*. Jesus linked the love of God to the service of neighbor. The four frames in **ILLUSTRATION 25B** show Sylvester growing in his understanding of Jesus' teaching.

 He learns that the Christian faith speaks about loving God and others. However, he is not sure how much he should love God and others (***question marks, percentage marks***), and he does not understand that the so-called *two* commandments are really *one*.

 Sylvester makes up his mind to serve God "***100%***"—and feels a little smug about it (***halo***). However, he is not sure how much effort he should put into loving and serving those around him (***question mark and percentage mark on arrow to neighbor***).

 God teaches Sylvester that, if he wishes to devote life to the service of God, he must dedicate life to the service of others. The *two* commandments are *one* and *inseparable*. God's people are to devote life ***100%*** to the worship and service of God by devoting it ***100%*** to the service of ***neighbor***.

 The *first commandment* tells us how God would have us develop life under Him and use it for Him (***"1" on law-codes***). The *second commandment* tells us what we are to do for God in the service of others (***"2" on law-codes***). We are to use life to help others become what God has helped us become. There is no third set of laws (***law-codes with three sections and "3" canceled out***) that speaks of duties to self.

In 1 Corinthians 11:27–29, Paul writes:

> *Whoever, therefore, eats the bread or drinks the cup of the Lord in an unworthy manner will be answerable for the body and blood of the Lord. Examine yourselves, and only then eat of the bread and drink of the cup. For all who eat and drink without discerning the body, eat and drink judgment against themselves.*

Much discussion has taken place about what Paul means by "unworthy manner," "examine," "without discerning the body." We can understand what Paul means when we know something about the situation to which he was writing.

In the early church, Christians used to gather for community meals (called *love feasts*). They often celebrated the Lord's Supper at the conclusion of these meals. Bad things were happening at these observances in Corinth. Rich people brought lots of food, but kept to themselves, did not share their food, and overate. Poor people brought little or nothing, and were left to themselves and their hunger. Paul accuses the rich of behaving in an "unworthy manner," and of failing to "examine" themselves concerning their responsibilities to other members of the Lord's "body" or family. (See also First Corinthians 11:33,34.)

ILLUSTRATION 25C and **ILLUSTRATION 25D** relate this matter to the life of God's people today.

In the Lord's Supper we celebrate the truth that Jesus has given Himself for us, has forgiven us, and gives us eternal fellowship with Himself. Our celebration motivates us to respond. Toward the close of our worship we offer a prayer, such as:

> *We give thanks to you, Almighty God, that you have refreshed us through this saving gift, and we implore you that of your mercy you would strengthen us through the same in faith towards you and in fervent love to one another; through Jesus Christ, your Son, our Lord, who lives and reigns with you and the Holy Spirit, one God, now and forever.*

People today tend to confuse the biblical word *love* with the word *like*. However, God does not command us to *like* people, but to *love* them. The English language uses the one word *love* to express several Greek words, four of which are depicted in **ILLUSTRATION 25C**.

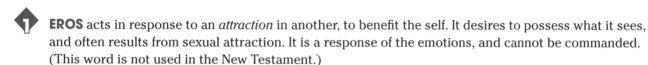 **EROS** acts in response to an *attraction* in another, to benefit the self. It desires to possess what it sees, and often results from sexual attraction. It is a response of the emotions, and cannot be commanded. (This word is not used in the New Testament.)

 **PHILIA** refers to *friendship*, such as the companionship that existed between David and Jonathan, 1 Samuel 18:1–4.

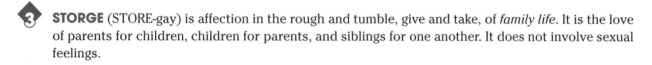 **STORGE** (STORE-gay) is affection in the rough and tumble, give and take, of *family life*. It is the love of parents for children, children for parents, and siblings for one another. It does not involve sexual feelings.

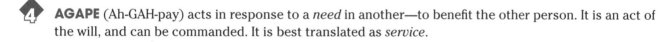 **AGAPE** (Ah-GAH-pay) acts in response to a *need* in another—to benefit the other person. It is an act of the will, and can be commanded. It is best translated as *service*.

The Bible uses the word *agape* to speak of God's love for humanity, and the love people are to have for one another. It follows, then, that through the celebration of the Lord's Supper, God seeks to increase His people's commitment to serve God and others.

The desired outcome of the celebration is well expressed in another closing prayer which reminds us that, as we grow in years, God wants us to use life more and more as Jesus used His.

> *Almighty God, you gave your Son both as sacrifice for sin and a model for the godly life. Enable us to receive Him always with thanksgiving and to conform our lives to His; through the same Jesus Christ our Lord.*

Another closing prayer points to God's plan to unite humanity around Jesus.

> *Pour out upon us the spirit of love, O Lord, and unite the wills of those whom you have fed with one heavenly food; through Jesus Christ our Lord.*

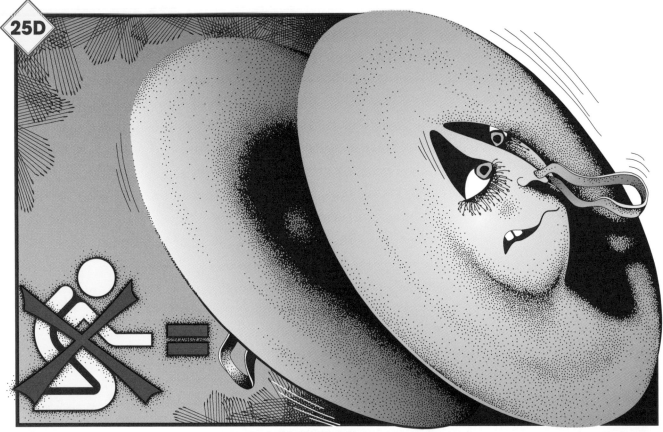

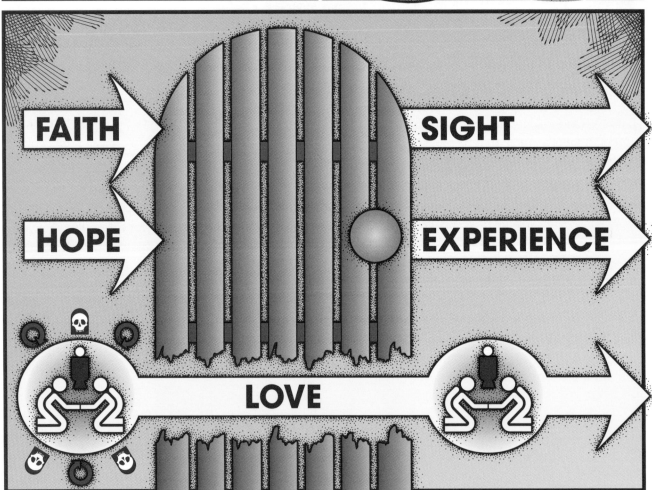

ILLUSTRATION 25D depicts the profound significance of Paul's message in 1 Corinthians 13:1–13.

Upper section

In this chapter, Paul discusses spiritual gifts. He points out that a person may speak in tongues with great eloquence, have great prophetic power and vast knowledge, understand all mysteries, and possess a faith strong enough to move mountains. However, all this is worthless and pointless unless that person uses life to serve others. The person who is full of religious talk but does not serve others is all noise (**servant figure canceled out**; *clanging cymbal*).

Lower section

In 1 Corinthians 13:4–7, Paul describes love's qualities, and in vv. 8–13 stresses that love will continue throughout this life and the next. Finally, in v. 13, Paul writes that *faith*, *hope*, and *love* (i.e., *service*) persist and endure, but the greatest of these three gifts of the Spirit is *love*. Why is love the greatest?

◆ **FAITH** (1 Corinthians 13:13) means *believing in things we cannot see*. However, after death (***door with slats***), we shall *see* God and the eternal world. *Faith* will give way to **SIGHT**.

◆ **HOPE** means looking forward to things to come. However, beyond death *hope* will give way to **EXPERIENCE**.

◆ **LOVE** will not cease. It is God's greatest gift, in that it will ***transcend death*** and will ***continue on into the life to come***.

In relation to the eternal nature of love, the illustration depicts two people (***two servant figures inside a circle***, ***symbols of the Lord's Supper above and between them***, *left*). Around them "in this present world" are ***symbols of sin and death***. An ***arrow labeled LOVE***, points to the right and passes through death (***door with slats***) into eternity where a ***second circle with the symbols of servanthood and heavenly meal is depicted once again***.

The eternal realm has broken into this present evil age. God's people are to live to serve God and others! They are to live *now* as they will *in heaven forever*.

25A There are different views in Christendom regarding what a worshiper eats and drinks in the celebration of the Lord's Supper. Some believe that the bread and wine are changed into Jesus' body and blood. Some teach that the bread and wine are symbols of Jesus' presence in our midst. Some profess that together with bread and wine, Jesus gives us His true spiritual body and blood.

25B Participation in the celebration of the Lord's Supper is a joyous event, yet one that is not to be taken lightly. Those who know they are most unworthy to participate are, ironically, most worthy to do so. At the same time, those who celebrate Jesus' love for them are to demonstrate their faith throughout life in loving service to others.

25C The English language uses the word *love* in a number of ways. Some confuse *love* with *like*, and are troubled that they find it hard to like certain individuals. God does not command us to *like* anyone, but to *love* everyone. To *love* another is to *serve* that person.

25D Through faith in Jesus the Messiah, we Christians already belong to God's eternal realm. In the Lord's Supper, we celebrate our citizenship in that realm. Participation in this heavenly celebration moves us to live on earth as the united, loving family that we shall one day be in heaven.

THE DIVINE DRAMA®

OUR NARRATIVE

UNIT 26

Kingdoms in Conflict

 When Jesus' work on earth was completed, He "ascended into heaven," Acts 1:9 (*glorified Jesus ascending*, *upper center*). However, Jesus did not *withdraw* His presence; He *transformed* it.

 When Jesus ascended, He gave *parting gifts* to God's people. Those parting gifts were persons of the Word: "apostles, prophets, evangelists, pastors and teachers," Ephesians 4:11. In **ILLUSTRATION 26A**, these parting gifts are depicted as *clergy*, superimposed on *gift boxes*, complete with an open *Bible*. These *persons of the Word* have a *servant role* (*servant figures on Bibles*)—to study, proclaim, and teach Jesus' Word.

 The role of Jesus' "parting gifts" is not to *do the work of the Church for other people*, but to *reflect* Jesus' servant mind and mission in all they do, and to *equip* other people to *be* the church. According to Ephesians 4:12, their task is:

> to equip the saints for the work of ministry. (RSV, NRSV)

> to equip God's people for work in His service. (NEB)

> to prepare all God's people for the work of Christian service. (TEV)

Persons of the Word are not to serve *people's whims* but *Jesus' will*. Jesus writes their agenda; their members do not. They are to serve people, not as people might want to be served, but as Jesus wants them to be served.

Furthermore when Jesus' "parting gifts" do things to draw attention to themselves, they invalidate their ministry. The goal must always be to draw attention to Jesus, and to inspire and empower people to believe in and follow Jesus.

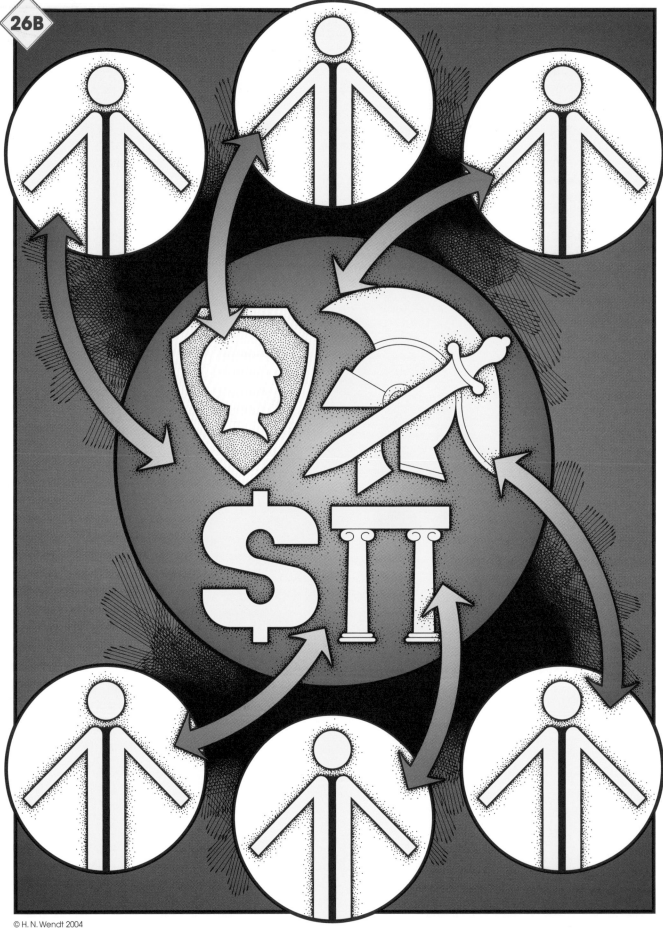

The Greek word which the New Testament translates as "church" is *ekklysia*. In the ancient Greek world, *ekklysia* was not used to refer to a building, or to a religious group or activity. It was the name given to the local governing body (e.g., council) which met in a Greek city or town to discuss local affairs, and to vote and act on them.

ILLUSTRATION 26B depicts this meaning and use. The ***figures in the small outer circles*** represent people serving on a town council. The ***symbols in the large inner circle*** depict some of the matters they might have discussed (*reading clockwise from upper left*):

◆ ***Face in profile:*** appointing a public official.

◆ ***Helmet and sword:*** protecting the realm.

◆ ***Pillars:*** constructing or repairing a building.

◆ ***Dollar sign:*** collecting local taxes

The ***double-headed arrows*** signify that after the officials *came together* to meet, discuss, and vote, they *went forth* to carry out their decisions.

26C

God's Church

The mention of the word "church" arouses in many minds the image of a building. The Bible, however, relates *church* to a *community of people in fellowship with Jesus*—never to a *building*.

ILLUSTRATION 26C depicts what the Bible means by the *church community*. The **symbol for God** is superimposed on **Planet Earth**—which God made and owns. People on Planet Earth work at many things. The symbols in the circles depict some of these (*reading counter-clockwise from upper center*):

◆ **Research chemist or pharmacist**

◆ **Janitor**

◆ **Farmer**

◆ **Engineer**

◆ **Musician**

The **circle** in the *upper right corner* has been left **empty** to permit people to write or sketch in their own occupation, or role in life at the present time.

God calls His people, His community, His church, into His presence (**double-headed arrows from people to God**) to tell them who God is, what God has made and owns (**Planet Earth**), and what God has done for them through Jesus the Messiah (**Servant-King, cross, open tomb, rising arrow** signifying Jesus' ascension). God then sends them back to live as God's people in whatever they do (**double-headed arrows point back to occupations and roles**).

God's will is that His people do everything, including their daily work, in a way that reflects the mind and manner of Jesus, the Servant Messiah.

26D

124

Sometimes people ask others, "Are you interested in religion?" The question reflects the idea that life can be divided up into:

◆ *Spiritual* interests—things that *have to do with religion.*

◆ *Secular* interests—things that *have nothing to do with religion.*

However, there is no *secular* world. God made and owns the universe. "We live and move and have our being" in God, Acts 17:28. If *God* does not control us, *Satan* does, 1 John 3:8; Matthew 6:24; Romans 8:12–14.

ILLUSTRATION 26D builds on **ILLUSTRATION 26C**. In it, ***Satan is at the center of life***, framed in the s**ymbol for sin**, self-centeredness, and self-service. The ***arms of the persons in the small circles*** are not raised in *praise* to God, but reflect an attitude of *indifference* to God.

We Christians find ourselves involved in a spiritual struggle, as both God (**ILLUSTRATION 26C**) and Satan (**ILLUSTRATION 26D**) desire to control our lives, Ephesians 6:10–18. The *presence* of the struggle should not perturb us; its *absence* should. Its presence indicates that our faith in Jesus the Messiah as Savior and Lord is alive, and that we are fighting a genuine warfare against the satanic realm.

C.S. Lewis once wrote:

> There is no neutral ground in the universe. Every square inch is claimed by God, and counterclaimed by Satan.

Lewis' words express the profound and challenging truth that **every person on the face of Planet Earth serves, worships, witnesses to, and supports either the work of God or the work of the demonic. These are the only options.**

Satan does not display himself as evil. He does not walk around with a large placard across his chest saying, "I am Satan. Let me teach you how to sin—how to do really bad things."

 Paul writes that Satan operates as an angel of light (2 Corinthians 11:14)—as it were, with a **pleasant smile** on his face. Satan tempts us with, "Come! Let me teach you how to live life to the fullest. It's all respectable and legal. **You are Number One.** You owe it to yourself. Enjoy the fruits of your success. Go here. Go there. Fork it down. Pour it down. Drink it up. Paint it on. Spray it on. Live it up. Have fun! There's no harm in it!"

Although the Bible says little about Satan's appearance, it says much about Satan's footprints across people's lives. To gain control of people, Satan does not need to persuade them to live openly *wicked* lives. He need only persuade them to live *useless, self-centered* lives, Matthew 25:14–30, especially vv. 24–30.

We Christians are constantly to remember that we are not here to live *comfortably*, but *usefully*, to the glory of God in the service of others in all we do—in ***government, education, eating, family life, use of money, leisure activities, daily work, and in church activities***.

In Romans 12:2a, Paul writes, "Do not be conformed to this world." J.B. Phillips (a British theologian) translates this verse, "Don't let the world around you squeeze you into its own mold."

ILLUSTRATION 26F depicts Phillips' translation. The pleasures, institutions, and occupations of this world place great pressure on people (like a **_clamp_**) to use them only for their own enjoyment and advancement (**_person caught inside symbol for sin_**). They pressure them to think, **_"I'm Number One!"_**

In his first letter, the apostle John writes:

> *Do not love the world or the things of the world. If anyone loves the world, love for the Father is not in him.* (1 John 2:15)

John is not suggesting that the created order is evil, and that therefore we are to cut ourselves off from it. God made the created order and declared it "good," Genesis 1. John's point is that *humanity is to use creation responsibly to glorify its Maker and Owner, and to benefit humanity*. To fail to do so is to serve that "god" called "covetousness," Ephesians 5:5; Colossians 3:5–10.

- ◆ The "world system" measures success by asking: *How much have I achieved for myself?*
- ◆ God's yardstick for measuring success is: *How much have you done for Me and others?*

The Church—the Body of Christ

The human body consists of many organs and members. The brain directs their movements. Although some of the body's members are visible and prominent, others are not—but none complains about not being on center stage, in the limelight. To gain some insights into how the body functions, do the following:

    a.   Raise your right arm parallel to the floor.

    b.   Raise your right thumb and wriggle it.

    c.   Use your right thumb to scratch your right thumb.

All goes well until "impossible c." Why?

No member of the human body can serve itself. Every member of the body lives to serve other members of the body. Furthermore, when one part of the body is injured, the rest of the body does not cut it off or out. It hurts with it, and works towards restoring it to health.

Paul refers to the church as "the body of Christ," Romans 12:1–8; 1 Corinthians 12; Ephesians 1:22,23; Colossians 2:19. Some understand the term to refer merely to the local congregation as a body, a group, a community of people. However, the term describes how God's people are to *function*.

 **ILLUSTRATION 26G** depicts God's church as a community of people possessing skills and abilities for use in a variety of occupations and situations (***symbols within body***).

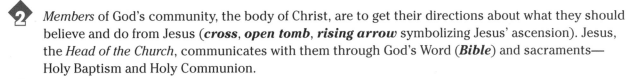 *Members* of God's community, the body of Christ, are to get their directions about what they should believe and do from Jesus (***cross***, ***open tomb***, ***rising arrow*** symbolizing Jesus' ascension). Jesus, the *Head of the Church*, communicates with them through God's Word (***Bible***) and sacraments— Holy Baptism and Holy Communion.

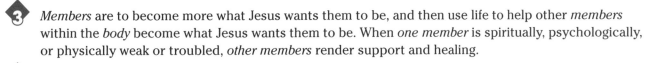 *Members* are to become more what Jesus wants them to be, and then use life to help other *members* within the *body* become what Jesus wants them to be. When *one member* is spiritually, psychologically, or physically weak or troubled, *other members* render support and healing.

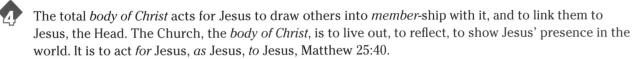 The total *body of Christ* acts for Jesus to draw others into *member*-ship with it, and to link them to Jesus, the Head. The Church, the *body of Christ*, is to live out, to reflect, to show Jesus' presence in the world. It is to act *for* Jesus, *as* Jesus, *to* Jesus, Matthew 25:40.

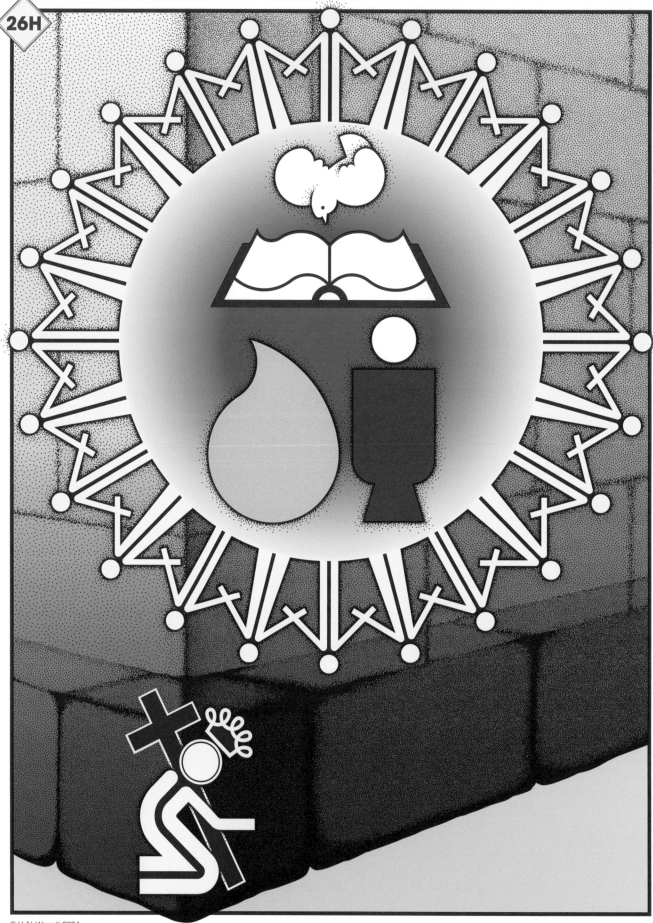

Earlier units make reference to the Tabernacle, the Tent of Meeting, Solomon's Temple, the Second Temple dedicated in 515 B.C., and Herod's Temple. What role does the concept of *Temple* play in the New Testament?

In John 1:51, Jesus says:

> Very truly, I tell you, you will see heaven opened and the angels of God ascending and descending upon the Son of Man.

Jesus' words are radical. Why?

 When Solomon built the Jerusalem Temple, he placed the Ark of the Covenant in the Holy of Holies. However, the Babylonians destroyed the Temple and the Ark in 587 B.C. Although the Jews who returned from Babylon rebuilt the Temple, the Ark no longer existed.

 However, the Holy of Holies in the Second Temple and in Herod's Temple was not empty. A low flat stone (called the *Foundation Stone*) was placed at the center of its floor. Each year on the Day of Atonement, the High Priest sprinkled the blood of a goat over this stone.

What was so special about this stone? Jewish teachers taught that Jacob had used it for a pillow while sleeping at Bethel when fleeing to Haran to escape the wrath of his brother Esau. While sleeping on it, Jacob had a dream in which he saw a ladder reaching up to heaven, with the angels of God ascending and descending on it. Furthermore, God spoke to Jacob that night, repeating to him promises God had made earlier to Abraham and Isaac, Genesis 28.

In Jesus' day, the Jews said that this stone was the place where God met humanity. It was the link between heaven and earth. Therefore, in John 1:51, Jesus says that He replaces the Holy of Holies and the Foundation Stone and its function. Jesus also said that He would replace the Temple complex as a whole with His "body" (John 2:19-22), by which Jesus meant His resurrected body and those Jesus gathers into fellowship with Himself.

 Peter says that the stones in the New Testament Temple are "*living* stones"—believers in Jesus, 1 Peter 2:5. Paul points out that God's people are God's Temple and dwelling place, 1 Corinthians 3:16; 2 Corinthians 6:16.

 In Ephesians 2:19-22, Paul describes the New Testament Temple as a *community of living stones*—of *people!* Jesus (**Servant-King carrying His cross**) is its **Cornerstone**. Just as a cornerstone determines the shape of a building, so Jesus determines the shape of God's New Testament Temple—or community. It is to be *servant-shaped*, for its Cornerstone is *servant-shaped*. The apostles and prophets, the first stones Jesus gathered into it, form its foundation. Jesus continues to gather *living stones* and to place them into God's Temple. This "dwelling place of God in the Spirit" will continue to grow until the Last Day, when it will be taken to heaven. There will be no Temple building in heaven (Revelation 21:22), for God will fill every corner of heaven, and God's people will dwell in His presence forever.

The New Testament Temple is a community of people among whom Jesus dwells, and to whom God speaks through Word and sacraments. Jesus' people show His presence among them through what they believe, say, and do.

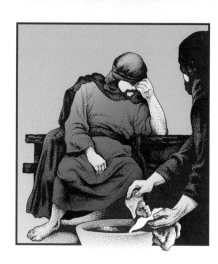

26A After Jesus completed His Messianic mission, Jesus withdrew His visible presence from among the disciples. However, down through the centuries, Jesus has given gifts to His people—persons who are to study, preach, and teach His Word to equip others for the work of Christian service.

26B In ancient Greece, the term *ekklysia* referred to groups entrusted with running the everyday affairs of a city, town, or region. After assembling for discussion and deciding on a course of action, its members went forth to carry out the decisions made in the meeting.

26C The New Testament uses the word *ekklysia* to describe Jesus' community, the Church. God summons people from every walk of life around God's presence to tell them who God is, what God has made and owns, and what God has done for their salvation. God then sends them back into their everyday life to use life as Jesus used His

26D If God is not at the center of our lives, Satan is.

26E Satan does not present himself as one who is evil and deadly, but as one whose only desire is to teach us how to enjoy life to the fullest—all for ourselves!

26F Satan works through the world system around us to exert a powerful pressure on us to live merely for our own sake.

26G In Holy Baptism, God grafts us into Jesus' *body*, or community. We are to serve one another within this community. Then, as Jesus' community, we are to serve the world around us in the spirit of Jesus.

26H The New Testament *Temple* is the Christian community. The risen Lord dwells among His people, speaking to them though His Word and sacraments, assuring them of His forgiving mercy, and encouraging them to serve one another and the world as He has served them.

THE DIVINE DRAMA®

OUR NARRATIVE

UNIT 27
The Privilege of Prayer

27A

In **ILLUSTRATION 27A**, one of the arrows protruding from the **symbol for God** extends down toward Sylvester in the lower left corner. Sylvester's hands are folded in prayer, and arrows (symbolizing praise and prayer) rise up from him toward God. Between God and Sylvester is the **Servant-King**—but with **hands raised in prayer** to denote that Jesus prays for His people, John 17:5–19. Jesus brings His brothers and sisters into the presence of His Father. Note the **symbol for sin beneath Jesus** and the **halo above Jesus' head**—to depict that God has done away with our "sin hat" through the cross of Jesus the Messiah, given us Jesus' sinless "holy hat" and declared us to be God's holy people, God's saints. Our prayer life is to reflect Jesus's prayer life—who, throughout His life, sought to glorify His Father, and to walk the way of a servant-without-limit.

The Privilege

 Dr. Charles Eliot once wrote:

> If you say there is no God, I can only ask how you—a speck of mortal living for a moment of time on an atom of an earth in plain sight of an infinite universe full of incredible beauty, wonder, and design—can so confidently hold so improbable a view.

We Christians not only *believe* that God exists, but we also *know* God as a Father and Friend through our relationship with God's Son, Jesus the Messiah. Although we cannot see God in His bare majesty, we know what God's heart is like for we have seen God in Jesus the Messiah, John 14:8,9.

 Paul twice says that Christians can pray to the Father as Jesus did, Romans 8:15; Galatians 4:6. On occasion, Jesus prayed "Abba, Father," Mark 14:36. In ancient Israel, small children used the word *Abba* when addressing their father. The only English word that conveys the true meaning of "Abba, Father" is *daddy*. How wonderful that we may speak with the creator, owner, and preserver of this vast universe and call Him "Our Father," Matthew 6:9.

The Practice

 God loves us, has forgiven us, and seeks fellowship with us, John 3:16; 1 Corinthians 1:2. We may approach God in prayer with confidence, Hebrews 4:16. Jesus gives us *access* into His presence (Romans 5:2; Ephesians 2:18; 3:12) and prays for us, Romans 8:34; Hebrews 9:24; 10:22.

 Prayer is talking *with* God rather than *to* God. If in prayer we merely speak *to* God, the danger is that we use prayer to tell God what *we want for ourselves*, rather than open ourselves to listen to God so that we might learn what *God is like*, and *what God wants for us and of us*.

 God speaks to us, and teaches us about God's love for us and His will for our lives, through His Word. God's children need to *listen to God* by studying and meditating on God's Word, Psalm 119:15,16. Those who *listen to God* in prayerful meditation understand much better what they should *speak to God* about, Colossians 3:17.

 God does not need our prayers; God can survive very well without them. God urges us to pray *for our sake*, for God knows *we need Him*. God's concern is not *God's ego*, but *our welfare*.

27B

Jesus is the *final teacher* about the practice of prayer, and Jesus' example is the *divine model* of the use of prayer.

The Practice

 In John 16:23; Jesus says to His disciples,

> *If you ask the Father for anything in My name, He will give it to you.* (NEB)

 Some look on the words *in Jesus' name* as almost a magic formula to extract from God whatever they want for themselves. However, to pray in Jesus' name means to commit ourselves to *learning* what God wants us to believe and *doing* what God wants us to do.

 In Jesus' name is not a term of *manipulation*, but one of (identification.) When we pray in Jesus' name, we ask that we might use our life as Jesus used life, and that Jesus' goals might become our goals.

 In Philippians 2:5–7, Paul writes:

> *Let the same mind be in you that was in Christ Jesus, who, although He was in the form of God, did not regard equality with God as something to be exploited, but emptied himself, taking the form of a slave.*

ILLUSTRATION 27B depicts the *mind of Christ Jesus* in the upper left-hand corner. The person below prays that the mind of Jesus will be reflected more and more in her mind and actions. She prays for guidance and power to use her life as Jesus used His.

The Promise

 Jesus promises that prayers *in His name* will be granted, "… He will give it to you," John 16:23. In Matthew 7:7,8 Jesus says:

> *Ask, and it will be given you; search, and you will find; knock, and the door will be opened to you. For everyone who asks receives, everyone who searches finds, and for everyone who knocks, the door will be opened.*

 God answers *all* prayer. God's answers include: "Yes," "No," "Later," and "Let's do it my way" (and perhaps sometimes, "You've got to be kidding!")

 If at times we feel our prayers are unanswered, we need to ask, "Did I pray to be empowered to live more *comfortably*, or to be inspired to live more *usefully*, as a Christ-like servant?"

 It is helpful to compare Matthew 7:11 with Luke 11:13. The "good things" referred to in Matthew are interpreted as "the Holy Spirit" in Luke. God always says "Yes!" to people who pray for help to understand Jesus' person and teaching, and for help to pattern their lives on His.

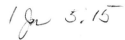

27C

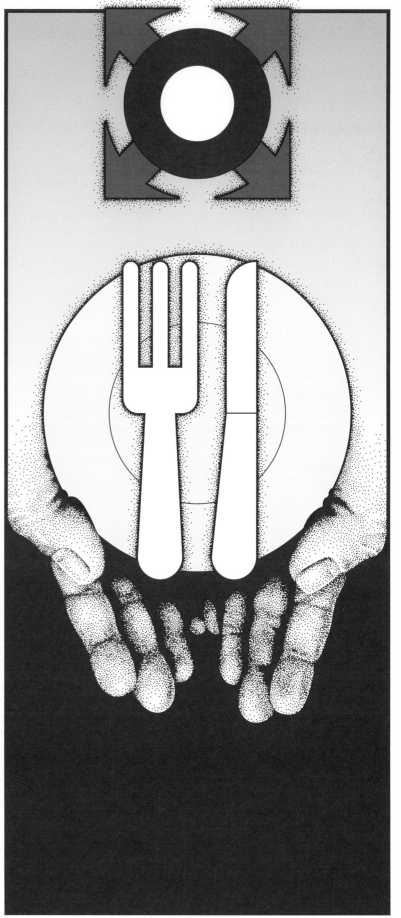

God Our Quartermaster

How do you react to the following story?

> *A young man has completed his military training, and has been posted overseas to a front-line position. As he gets ready to leave his parents and family, his father says to him, "Son, I think you'd better take along some cotton seed. You'll need a little cotton to produce some cloth to make yourself a uniform. And take a few cattle as well. There's nothing like a good barbecued steak once in awhile, and you'll need the leather to make yourself some boots. Don't forget to take along a few tools to make yourself a decent gun and some bullets."*

The story is invalid. When people go to a battlefront, they go there to locate the enemy and fight—with undivided attention. They do not have time to worry about supplies—and they do not have to. The quartermaster supplies their needs.

Left section

We Christians are constantly at God's *front line* in a full-time battle against Satan. We must study Satan's camouflages and strategies, and equip our minds to fight in Jesus' way by devoting life to serving God and others. We pray for God's guidance, inspiration, and power to reflect Jesus' mind and manner in all we do (***praying hands***, ***Servant-King***).

Right section

 We are not to worry about supplying our own needs. We do not need to, for God attends to that (***symbol for God; God's hands extended downward, with plate, knife, and fork***). God is our quartermaster. As we look to God for guidance and strength to fight Satan effectively, we also look to God to sustain our physical bodies.

 In Matthew 6:25, Jesus says:

> *Therefore I tell you, do not worry about your life, what you will eat or what you will drink, or about your body, what you will wear. Is not life more than food, and the body more than clothing?*

Jesus argues from the greater to the lesser. If God has given us such a precious thing as life, God will provide food to sustain that life. If God has given us the miracle of our body, God will provide clothing for that body. However, God will provide what God knows we need—not what the advertising world says we should eat and wear. God promises to supply our *needs*—not our *greeds.*

 In Matthew 6:33, Jesus tells us to strive *first* for God's kingdom and righteousness, and to rest assured that as we do that, God will provide our needs. The words "strive *first*" imply: *the one and only concern you are to have in life is…* Luke omits the word *first*, 12:31. In Matthew 4:10, Jesus says we are to worship and serve *only* God. We are to busy ourselves fighting God's battle (using creation and life to serve God and others), and to leave it to God to supply what God knows we need.

 When people have much more than they need, the issue is not that God has singled them out for special blessing. It is that they have not cared for, and shared with, a needy world. Although God has *provided* for humanity's needs, humanity has not *divided* justly and equitably what God supplies!

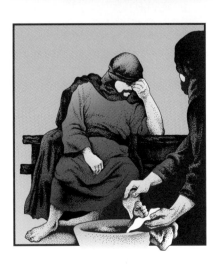

27A In prayer, we talk *with* God—*with* God because we both *listen to* God and *speak with* God. We listen to God by reading and meditating on God's Word. Because of what Jesus has done for us, we are able to approach God with joy and confidence.

27B We pray *in Jesus' name*. This implies that we have access to God through Jesus the Messiah, and that the things we pray about are to reflect the things Jesus prayed about. We ask God to help us develop and demonstrate Jesus' attitude towards His Father, the created order, and other people.

27C We should not pray to God with unnecessary and sinful requests—for example, to provide us with an excess of material goods to enjoy. We leave it to God to provide our *needs* rather than our *greeds*. Our central concern is to ask God to empower us to walk Jesus' way, and to fight an effective battle against Satan, the world order, and our own sinful desires.

THE DIVINE DRAMA®

OUR NARRATIVE

UNIT 28
The Lord's Prayer

POWER
POSITION
PROFIT
PLEASURE

ILLUSTRATION 28A depicts the two realms or kingdoms that seek to control our lives. It builds on **ILLUSTRATION 26C** and **ILLUSTRATION 26D**.

Upper section

The Kingdom of God

The Kingdom of God does not have geographical borders. It consists of people who live in faith and obedience under God as King (**crown**, **symbol for God**, **servant figure**, *right segment*). These people serve God and others in thought, word, and deed.

*Our citizenship in God's Kingdom is brought about by Jesus the Messiah (**glorified Jesus**, left segment).* Jesus works through His Holy Spirit (**dove**) who in turn uses God's Word and sacraments (**Bible, symbols for Holy Baptism and the Lord's Supper**) to bring us to saving faith in Jesus the Messiah, and to membership in God's eternal family. *The entry point in God's Kingdom is Jesus' redeeming cross and victory over death (**arrow pointing from left segment to right segment; cross, open tomb**).*

Lower section

The Kingdom of the Devil, the World, and our Flesh

◆ The Bible frequently refers to Satan, 1 Chronicles 21:1; Matthew 4:1–11; 1 Peter 5:8,9; Revelation 12:9 (**Satanic face**, *left segment*). *The demonic is every person, power, institution, and pressure that would sidetrack us from living to serve God and others into living to serve ourselves.*

◆ Satan works through the *world order* (**Planet Earth with words superimposed**) and the *sinful human heart* (**symbol for sin, law-codes, human heart**) to persuade people to live for themselves—but really for Satan. Satan suggests all that matters is **POWER** *for self*, **POSITION** *for self*, **PROFIT** *for self*, and **PLEASURE** *for self*.

◆ Those who live under Satan reject God as King of their lives, and adopt an indifferent or arrogant attitude toward God (**crown and symbol for God canceled out, person in posture of indifference, symbol for sin**, *right segment*).

◆ Note the **arrow pointing from the left segment to the right segment**. In the *left segment* are symbols of the "deadly trio" (*Satan, world order, sinful heart*). In the *right segment* are symbols of the influence the deadly trio want to have on human life. Satan is quite happy to have people live *decent* lives as the world judges *decency*—as long as they do not overdo it, and as long as they think their "good deeds" make them acceptable to God.

Both kingdoms depicted in **ILLUSTRATION 28A** struggle for control of the lives of Christians. **The Kingdom of God is present only *imperfectly* in Christians in this life; it will be present *perfectly* only in heaven.**

THE LORD'S PRAYER IN THE NEW TESTAMENT

◆ Two Gospels tell of the origin of the Lord's Prayer, Matthew 6:9–13, Luke 11:1–4. In Matthew, Jesus gives it as a pattern for prayer rather than as words to be repeated ("Pray then *like this*," 6:9). In giving His prayer, Jesus urges the disciples to avoid display, wordiness, and pointless requests in their prayer life. In Luke, Jesus gives the prayer when the disciples ask Jesus to teach them to pray, as John had taught his disciples, 11:1,2.

◆ Some suggest that while the first three and the last three petitions ask for *spiritual* things, the fourth petition ("Give us this day our daily bread") asks for *material* things. However, all petitions ask for *Spirit*-ual things, namely, that God the Holy Spirit might empower us to reflect Jesus' attitudes and actions in all we think, say, and do. We pray that our lives will demonstrate Jesus' attitude towards His Father, the created order, and other people.

◆ **In the Lord's Prayer, we do not instruct God, but rather ask God to instruct us. We do not pray to inform God, but pray that God might reform us. We ask God to teach and empower us to serve God and others—in the spirit of Jesus the Messiah, our Savior and Lord.**

◆ Each petition uses few words to express profound truths about what God wants to happen in *our lives*, and how God wants to use us to influence *the lives of others*.

THE CONTENTS OF THE LORD'S PRAYER

The traditional version of the Lord's Prayer is:

> *Our Father, who art in heaven,*
> *Hallowed be Thy name;*
> *Thy kingdom come,*
> *Thy will be done,*
> > *on earth as it is in heaven.*
> *Give us this day our daily bread;*
> *And forgive us our trespasses,*
> > *as we forgive those who trespass against us;*
> *Lead us not into temptation,*
> *But deliver us from evil.*
> > *For Thine is the kingdom, and the power, and the glory forever and ever.*
> *Amen.*

In what follows, the wording is from the NRSV translation of Matthew 6:9–13.

INTRODUCTION: *Our Father in Heaven*

 We pray, "*Our* Father"—not, "*My* Father." We bring before God the needs of all people, as well as our own, 1 John 3:14–18.

 We approach God with confidence as "Our *Father*," knowing that God wants only our good, for God is the Source and Sustainer of all, Psalm 100.

 We pray with trust "*in heaven*," not to suggest that God is *distant*, but to confess that God is *different* from earthly fathers. God's power and wisdom know no limits, and God's loving concern for our welfare never varies, Psalm 103:1–5.

PETITION 1: *Hallowed be Your name*

1 To *hallow* is to treat as holy, to respect and hold in awe, to revere a person as that person deserves to be treated. In this petition, *name* does not refer to one of God's titles or *name tags*, but to God as God is, Leviticus 24:16; John 17:6.

2 In the first petition we pray that, through His Word, God will:

    a. Teach us to know God as maker, owner, sustainer, and Lord of creation, and to give God the respect, gratitude, and obedience due to God.

    b. Enlighten us to detect and reject every satanic lie.

    c. Use us to influence others to hallow God.

PETITION 2: *Your kingdom come*

1 If God's Kingdom prevailed everywhere on earth, there would be no point in praying these words. However, on earth the kingdom of the *deadly trio* holds many in its power.

2 We pray that, through His Word, God might enlighten us—and others through us—to understand the nature of the two kingdoms, to flee Satan's kingdom, and submit to God's Kingdom. Furthermore, we commit ourselves to work toward drawing other people into God's Kingdom.

PETITION 3: *Your will be done*

1 We ask God to help us, through His Word, to know and distinguish between *God's will*, and the *will of the deadly trio of Satan, the world, and the flesh*.

2 We ask God to equip us—and others through us—to know and submit to God's will for our lives.

REFRAIN: *on earth as it is in heaven*

1 These words are meant to be applied to each of the first three petitions, whose messages then are:

    Hallowed be Your Name *on earth as it is in heaven.*
    Your kingdom come *on earth as it is in heaven.*
    Your will be done *on earth as it is in heaven.*

2 These words remind us that where God is in complete control ("in heaven"), all is well. There God's name is hallowed, God's kingdom prevails, and God's will is done. However, "on earth" the deadly trio of Satan, the world order, and sinful flesh (corrupt human nature) strive to mislead humanity. (**ILLUSTRATION 28A** depicts the two realms, the struggle between them, and the goal that each seeks.) We pray, then, that things *on earth* may become increasingly more as they are *in heaven.*

PETITION 4: *Give us this day our daily bread*

1 The term *daily bread* means all we need each day to sustain and support life.

2 God gives (*supplies*) our daily bread (*needs*) whether we ask or not, whether we thank God or not. God will continue to do so.

3 In the fourth petition, we ask God to give us awareness and gratitude: *awareness* of the origin of *our* daily bread, and *gratitude* to the Giver (supplier). God supplies our needs as a by-product of our daily work, which God also provides and empowers.

Because God assures us that God is the *quartermaster* (**ILLUSTRATION 27C**) who supplies our needs, our trust in God frees us from unnecessary earthly concerns. We can devote ourselves to the service of others—and therefore God!

 In praying *us* and *our*—rather than *me* and *my*—we commit ourselves to be God's instruments to supply the needs of all who live on this global village called Planet Earth.

PETITION 5: *Forgive us our debts, as we also have forgiven our debtors*

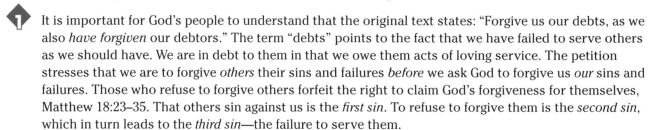 It is important for God's people to understand that the original text states: "Forgive us our debts, as we also *have forgiven* our debtors." The term "debts" points to the fact that we have failed to serve others as we should have. We are in debt to them in that we owe them acts of loving service. The petition stresses that we are to forgive *others* their sins and failures *before* we ask God to forgive us *our* sins and failures. Those who refuse to forgive others forfeit the right to claim God's forgiveness for themselves, Matthew 18:23–35. That others sin against us is the *first sin*. To refuse to forgive them is the *second sin*, which in turn leads to the *third sin*—the failure to serve them.

 In Jesus, God has already forgiven us. God has removed our sins as far from us as east is from west, Psalm 103:12. God's goal is now to help us become more what God wants us to be—like Jesus.

 Similarly, we are to forgive others the wrong they do to us, and devote ourselves to helping them become what *God* wants them to be—not what *they* want to be!

PETITION 6: *Do not bring us to the time of trial*

 God tempts no one to sin, James 1:13–15. However, God permits us to encounter many situations and difficulties designed to keep our spiritual muscles strong. For example, when sickness and adversity strike others, God gives us an opportunity to be *little Christs* to the helpless. When sickness and adversity strike us, God gives us an opportunity to be the *helpless Christ* whom others can serve, Matthew 25:31–40.

 In this petition, we pray that God will help us deal with every situation in life in a way that is in keeping with God's will for us. We pray that, in our attitudes and actions, God might help us reflect the mind of Jesus in every situation, and use us to help others do the same.

PETITION 7: *But deliver us from evil*, or *But rescue us from the Evil One*

 The Greek text of this passage (Matthew 6:13) permits either translation. The first views evil broadly, as undesirable experiences. The second asks for deliverance from the satanic realm at work in the world. If the second translation is accepted, the sixth and seventh petitions form a unit that says, "In the tests that come to us throughout life, help us to know and do God's will, and deliver us from Satan's temptations to do his will."

 "Deliver us from the Evil One" forms a fitting conclusion to the Lord's Prayer. Jesus looks back over all the noble things He asks us to pray about, and urges us to remember that our walk through life will never be easy. The enemy is around. Although society often treats Satan as a comic-strip character, Jesus exhorts us to view Satan very differently (John 8:44; 1 Peter 5:8,9), and to urge others to do so also.

CONCLUSION: *For Yours is the kingdom, and the power, and the glory, forever and ever. Amen.*

The closing words of the Lord's Prayer ("For Yours is the kingdom, and the power, and the glory, forever and ever") reflect 1 Chronicles 29:11. They are found in some ancient New Testament manuscripts as well.

Amen is a Hebrew word meaning *truly, truly,* or *certainly, certainly.* It denotes that God gladly hears the kinds of petitions we offer in the Lord's Prayer. Furthermore, God earnestly desires to bring them to pass in our lives—and in the lives of others, through us.

28A In all that we do, we are motivated and directed either by our gracious, forgiving God (the kingdom of God) or by the trio of Satan, the world order, and our own sinful flesh (the kingdom of Satan).

Non-Christians are controlled by the second kingdom.
In Christians, the kingdom of God and the kingdom of Satan both struggle for control; the struggle ceases only at death.

The Lord's Prayer

In praying the Lord's Prayer, we acknowledge the existence of both kingdoms. Furthermore, we ask God to enlighten us concerning their goals and methods, and to empower us to flee Satan's kingdom and to submit only to God's Kingdom. We also ask God to use us to draw others from Satan's kingdom into God's kingdom.

THE DIVINE DRAMA

OUR NARRATIVE

UNIT 29
Redeemed to Be Responsible

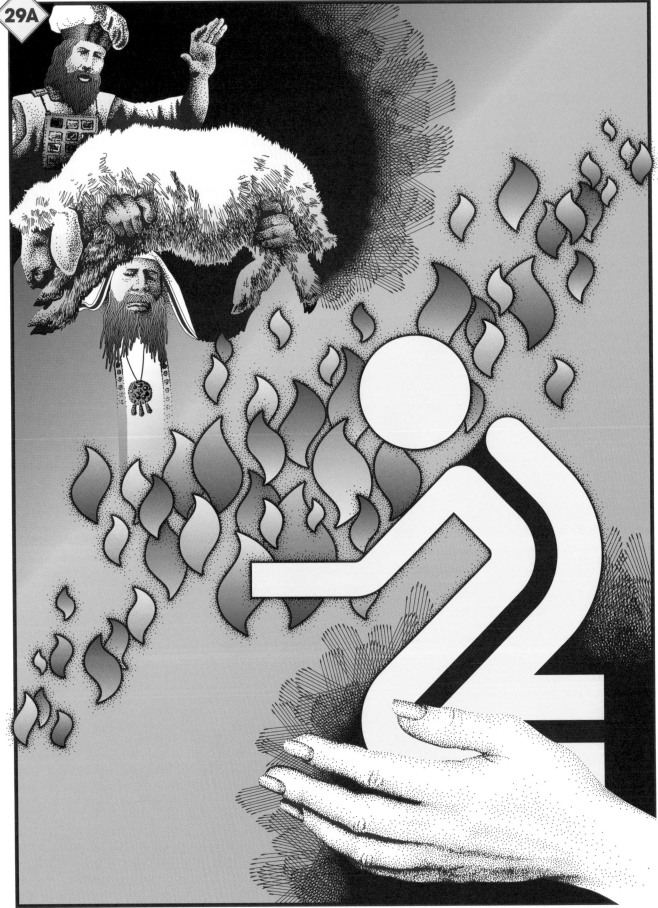

ILLUSTRATION 29A shows the difference between the *Old Testament sacrificial system*, and the *New Testament sacrificial system*.

Upper left section

In Old Testament times, the Israelites offered a variety of sacrifices, including animal sacrifice (***sheep***), in numerous shrines in Israel. Some of these were burnt (***flames***) by the officiating ***priests*** on an altar at the shrine. There is reason to believe that beyond the time of King Josiah's reform in 621 B.C., sacrifices could be offered only in the Jerusalem Temple.

The prophets, who worked prior to the Babylonian destruction of Jerusalem and Judah in 587 B.C., attacked the sacrificial system. They insisted that the practice of the sacrificial system was meaningless unless God's people cared for the widow, the orphan, and the needy, Isaiah 1:10–17. Several of the prophets suggest that God had not even commanded the Israelites to offer sacrifices, Amos 5:25; Jeremiah 7:21–23 (RSV and NRSV translations).

Lower right section

Although Jesus' parents took Him to Jerusalem each year (until Jesus was 12 years of age, Luke 2:41,42) for the Passover observances, we never read of Jesus offering sacrifice during His earthly ministry. Jesus insisted that what mattered was the practice of mercy toward others, not the offering of sacrifice, Hosea 6:6, Matthew 9:13, 12:7.

The New Testament states that we are to offer our living bodies to God by devoting life, in the spirit of Jesus, to the service of those around us (***servant figure in extended hand***). Paul wrote:

> *I appeal to you, therefore, brothers and sisters, by the mercies of God, to present your bodies as a living sacrifice, holy and acceptable to God, which is your spiritual worship.* (Romans 12:1)

> *Christ died for all, so that those who live might no longer live for themselves, but for Him who died and was raised for them.* (2 Corinthians 5:15)

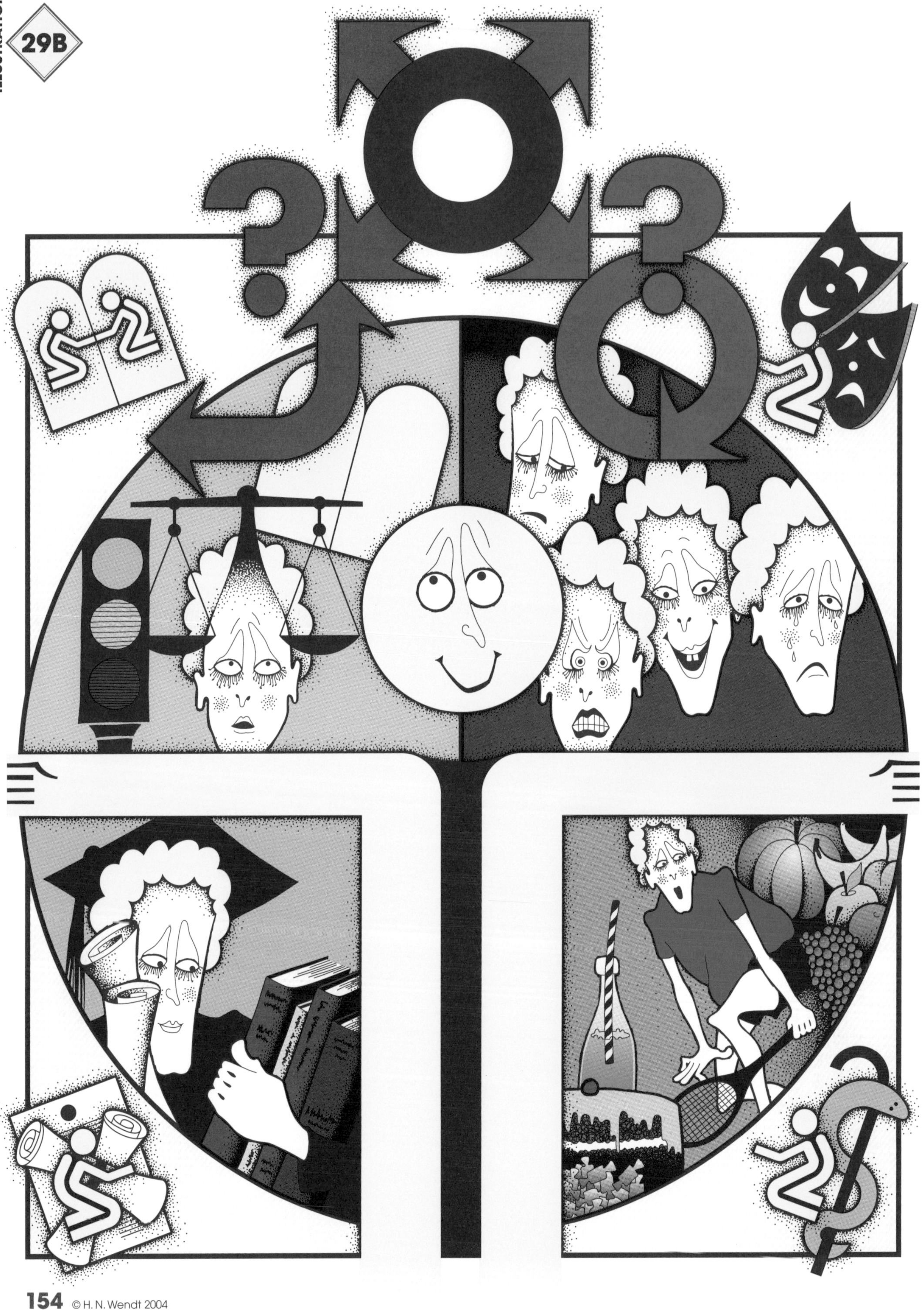

God made us. God owns us. God endows us with abilities. God wants us to care for, and develop, ourselves for use as God's instruments in the service of others.

ILLUSTRATION 29B depicts in yellow a ***person's face and upper body, with arms and fingers extended***. The person is depicted within a ***circle divided into four segments*** representing people's volitional, emotional, physical, and intellectual powers. Under the ***symbol for God*** is a ***double-headed arrow*** denoting service to God and neighbor, and the ***symbol for sin***—with a ***question mark*** near each. The question marks ask, "Who is directing our walk through life? God (*left*), or the power of sin (*right*)?"

When Jesus engaged in a debate with a lawyer, the lawyer defined God's will for humanity as follows:

> *You shall love the Lord your God with all your* heart, *and with all your* soul, *and with all your* strength, *and with all your* mind; *and your neighbor as yourself.* (Luke 10:25–27)

Jesus not only *agreed* with him, but told him to *do* these things. The segments within the large circle contain symbols designed to help us understand the terms *heart*, *soul*, *strength*, and *mind*.

 Heart (*upper left segment*)

The term "heart" refers to our volitional powers. "With all your heart" means "with all your will." God wants us to have an informed will (***law-codes***) equipped to weigh moral issues (***balance*** or ***scales***). As with a ***traffic light***, God wants us to know when not to proceed (***red***), when to proceed with caution (***amber***), and when to proceed with a good conscience (***green***). God's will for us is that we learn to reflect Jesus' servant life in all that we do (***servant figure on law-codes***).

 Soul (*upper right segment*)

God wants to empower us to develop a Christ-like *demeanor* that attracts others to us, equips us to serve them, and creates unity within our immediate and extended community. Our happy external demeanor (***smiling face-mask***) reflects our inner disposition and helps establish links between us and others, and makes them more willing to listen to any witness that we might wish to make to them. An unhappy external demeanor (***unhappy face-mask***) creates barriers between us and others. The ***faces within the segment itself*** reflect a variety of moods and dispositions.

 Strength (*lower right segment*)

The segment contains symbols of ***fruits***, ***cake***, ***candy***, and ***drink***, and a ***person playing tennis***. God wants us to eat and drink healthfully, and to exercise to keep fit. When we do that, our bodies are more likely to be instruments God can use to serve others (***servant figure***), rather than liabilities others must serve. God has also empowered people to provide health care to those in need of it (***serpent around staff***, Numbers 21:4–9).

 Mind (*lower left segment*)

God wants us to study things that will edify us, and equip us to serve others better (***graduation hat***, ***diplomas***, ***books***).

God writes the agenda for our actions. We serve others as *God* wants us to serve them—not as *we* might want to serve them, or as *they* might want to be served. "You shall love your neighbor as yourself" does not mean "50% for others and 50% for me." God wants us to devote life 100% to serving God by serving others.

Our goal is to become more what God intends us to be, so that we might in turn help others become what God intends them to be.

29C

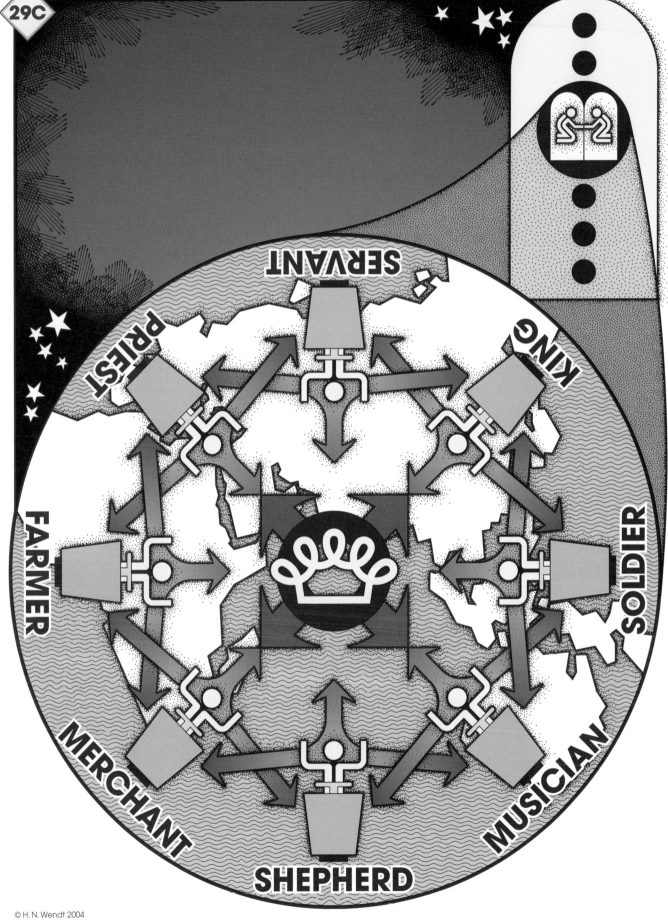

SERVANT

PRIEST

KING

FARMER

SOLDIER

MERCHANT

MUSICIAN

SHEPHERD

A Kingdom of Priests

The Priesthood Defined

1 After God gathered the Israelites around Mt. Sinai, God said to them, "Indeed, the whole earth is mine, but you shall be for me a priestly kingdom and a holy nation," Exodus 19:5b,6. God then made a covenant with them, Exodus 20.

2 In referring to them as a *priestly kingdom*, God did not mean that they were to do nothing but perform rituals in the Tabernacle and Temple. They were to live under God as their *King*, and to serve God as *priests* in all they did.

3 In this context, what is meant by the term *priest*? A priest is a person who:

    a.   Handles *sacred things*.

    b.   Goes *to God for others*, and *to others for God*.

4 What are *sacred things*? God says, "The whole earth is mine." Everything we touch has a *sacred quality*, for God made and owns all things.

5 All Christians are called to serve as God's priests full-time, in that they are called to use life full-time to glorify God and serve others.

The Priesthood Demonstrated

1 **ILLUSTRATION 29C** depicts *Planet Earth* with the **symbol for God** superimposed on it. God is King (**crown**) of the creation God made and owns.

2 Around God are **eight green pulpits**. **A person stands in each pulpit with arms raised in praise.** Beneath each pulpit is a **term denoting a calling in life**. *All* Christians, no matter what their calling, stand on *holy ground* and are in a *sacred situation* before God.

3 In the *upper right-hand corner* of **ILLUSTRATION 29C** is a **symbol for covenant**. At the **third dot** are the **law-codes**. As earlier units have pointed out, although Exodus–Deuteronomy contain 613 commandments (meant only for the Israelites), Jesus gives His followers a single commandment with two arms: they are to serve God full-time by serving others full-time (**an arrow goes up from each person in each pulpit to God, and is linked to arrows going sideways to neighbor**).

The loving service God's people render to others is to serve as a magnet to draw others into a relationship with God, Deuteronomy 4:1–8, especially vv. 6–8; John 13:34,35.

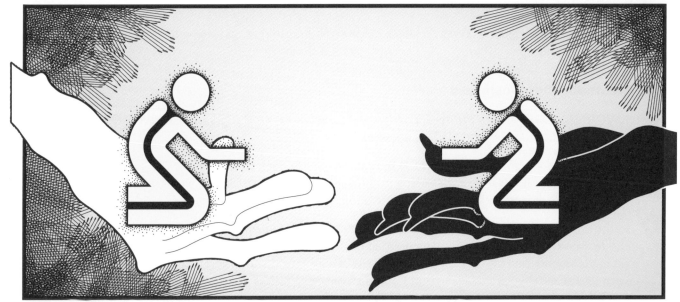

Money

ILLUSTRATION 29D deals with the following challenging questions:

◆ What is money?

◆ How are God's people are to understand the use of money?

Upper section

Mary, whose hand is on the left, grows apples. Mark, on the right, makes wheels for wheelbarrows. One day Mary gives Mark a wheelbarrow-load of ***apples***, and Mark gives Mary a new ***wheel*** for her wheelbarrow. What are they *giving* each other?

Although Mary put effort into growing them, the apples belong to God. The materials Mark used belong to God, and God supplied the knowledge and strength needed to make the wheel.

Middle section

In the final analysis, Mary and Mark exchange only the *effort* (***two servant figures***) that went into producing a barrow-load of apples and a wheel.

It is easier to see the apples as a gift of God rather than the wheel. However, every manufactured article might well bear the following label: "Raw materials—property of God; final product—fashioned by people using ingenuity and strength supplied by God."

Lower section

Perhaps one day Mary needs a wheel for her wheelbarrow, but Mark does not need any apples. Mary now gives him Christian effort, love, and service in a storable, exchangeable form—money (***dollar sign***). *Money is stored servanthood.*

Money itself is a lifeless thing, neither good nor bad. The Bible does not speak of *money* as the root of all evils. It speaks of the *love* of money as the root of all evils. Paul writes:

> *Of course, there is great gain in godliness combined with contentment; for we brought nothing into this world, so that we can take nothing out of it; but if we have food and clothing, we shall be content with these. But those who want to be rich fall into temptation and are trapped by many senseless and harmful desires that plunge people into ruin and destruction. For the love of money is a root of all kinds of evil, and in their eagerness to be rich some have wandered away from the faith and pierced themselves with many pains.* (1 Timothy 6:6–10)

> *So, whether you eat or drink, or whatever you do, do everything for the glory of God.* (1 Corinthians 10:31)

Christians are to do everything in a way that glorifies God and benefits others.

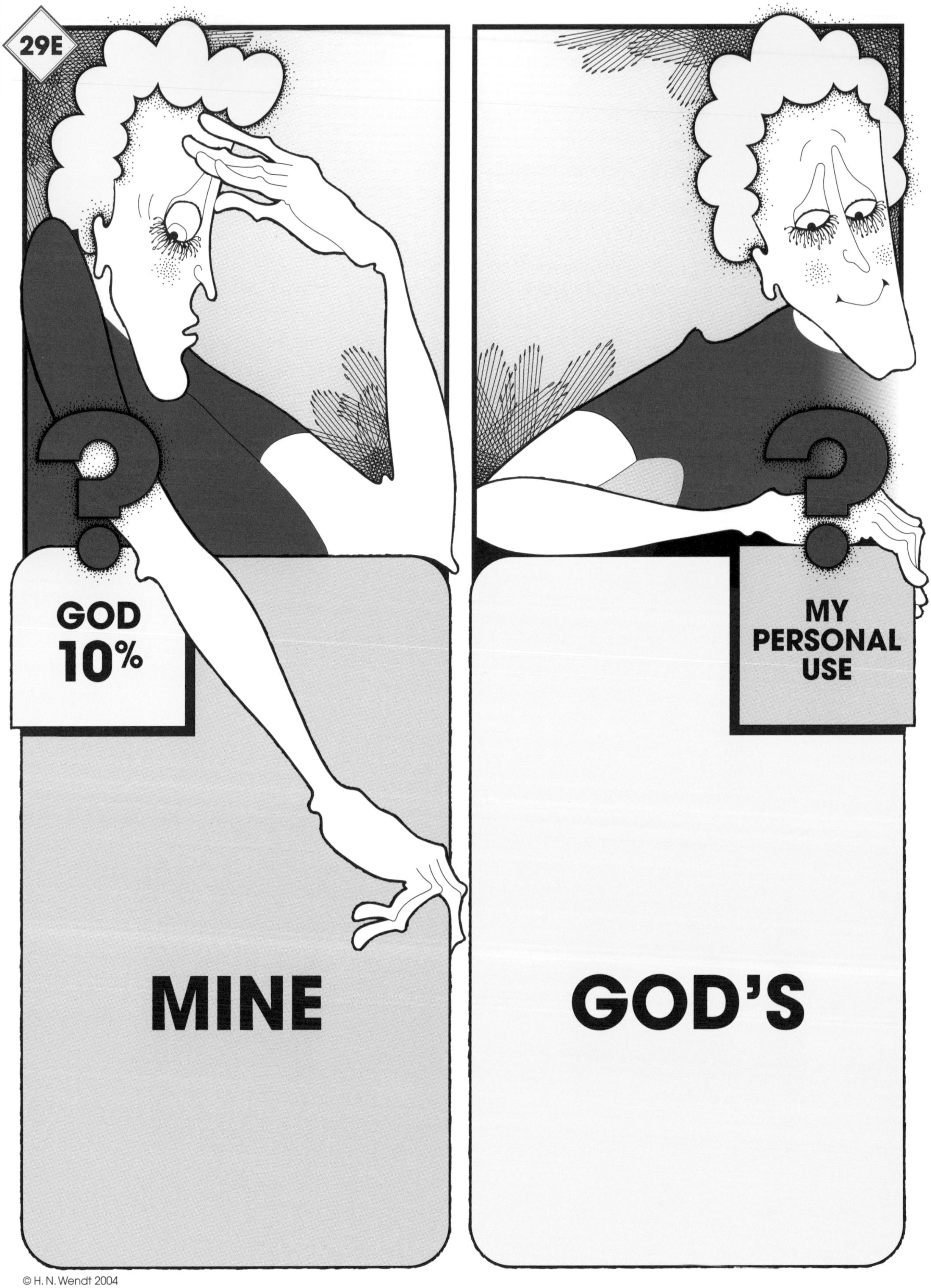
GOD
10%
MINE
MY
PERSONAL
USE
GOD'S

Left section

The Wrong Question

These days many people are bombarded with requests to "give" of *their Time, Talents, and Treasure* to help needy causes. They are sometimes challenged to think how much they should *give and use of their three T's* to the glory of God in the service of others.

ILLUSTRATION 29E depicts Sylvester assuming that those *three T's* are all his, and that he must decide what percentage he will *give* to God of what is *his* (**MINE**). No doubt, he assumes that after he has *given* his fair share to **GOD** (perhaps **10%**) , *the rest is his to do with as he pleases.*

Right section

The Right Question

Sylvester must change his question to, "How much of what belongs to God should I keep for **MY PERSONAL USE**. We make and own nothing. God made and owns everything, including the body we refer to as "mine," Exodus 19:5; Haggai 2:8; 1 Corinthians 4:7; Psalm 100; Deuteronomy 8. We humans are merely managers of **GOD'S** property. There is no such thing as *Christian giving*, for we cannot give what does not belong to us.

God's people are called to practice *Christian management and distribution*. When some of those among whom Paul had worked were thinking about what they might contribute toward the support of the needy in Jerusalem, they "gave *themselves* first to the Lord," 2 Corinthians 8:5. This enabled them to adopt God-pleasing attitudes. Their example preaches a powerful sermon to people in today's world.

POINTS TO PONDER

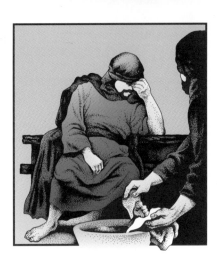

29A God has done, still does, and will continue to do many great and gracious things for us. God wants us to give something in return— our living bodies in the service of others.

29B God wants us to develop and care for our *volitional*, *emotional*, *physical*, and *intellectual* powers and abilities. God wants us to become what God intended us to be, so that we in turn can be better instruments for God to help others become what God intended them to be also.

29C God calls His people to be *priests* in all they do. As God's priests, they acknowledge that whatever they touch and use belongs to God. Furthermore, they seek to use creation and life to serve God and others.

29D Christians relate their use of creation and life, including their use of money, to God. They understand money to be *Christian service in a storable, exchangeable form*.

29E In "giving" money, Christians do not give of that which is theirs, but manage and distribute what God owns.

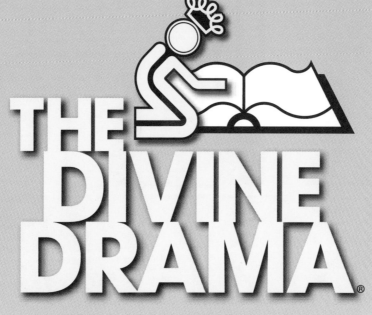

THE DIVINE DRAMA®

OUR NARRATIVE

UNIT 30
Therefore Beloved Brothers and Sisters

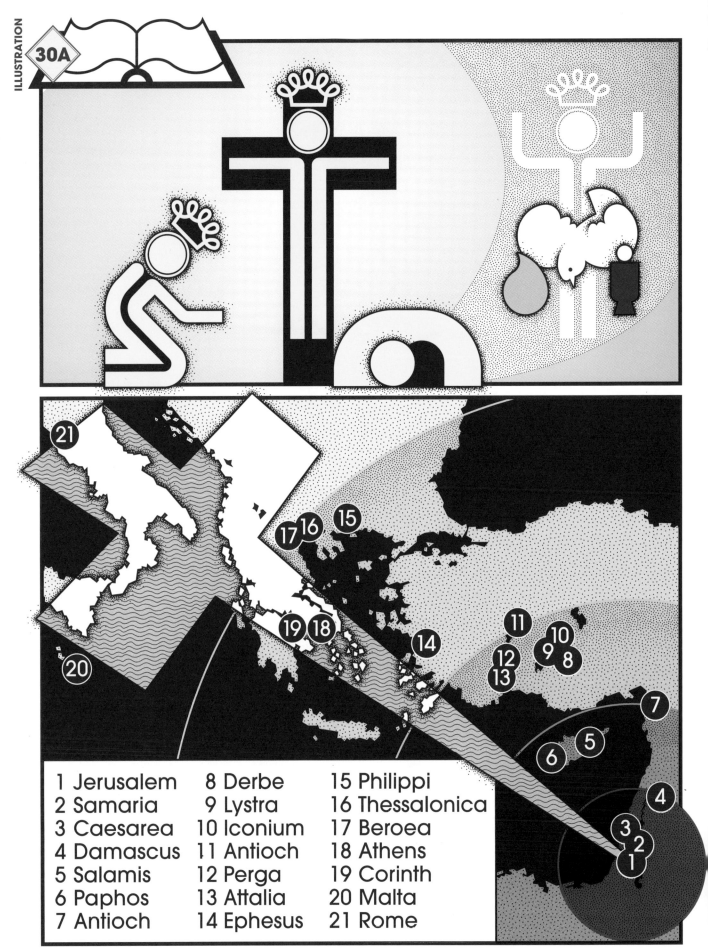

1 Jerusalem	8 Derbe	15 Philippi
2 Samaria	9 Lystra	16 Thessalonica
3 Caesarea	10 Iconium	17 Beroea
4 Damascus	11 Antioch	18 Athens
5 Salamis	12 Perga	19 Corinth
6 Paphos	13 Attalia	20 Malta
7 Antioch	14 Ephesus	21 Rome

Upper section

◆ Just before Jesus ascended into Heaven, He said to the disciples (now called apostles), "You shall be my witnesses in Jerusalem, and in all Judea and Samaria, and to the ends of the earth," Acts 1:8. Ten days later, the events of Pentecost empowered the apostles to begin their witness, Acts 2:1–42. Those present at that first Pentecost were Jews and proselytes (converts to Judaism)—not Gentiles. Joel 2:28,29, where the term "all flesh" refers to *Israelites, to Jews,* was being fulfilled—the Holy Spirit was being poured out on Abraham's descendants.

◆ The apostles proclaimed that God had fulfilled His promises to God's people. God had sent them their Messiah, Jesus of Nazareth (***Servant-King***), David's long-expected descendant, Acts 2:30.

◆ Because Jesus was a Servant-King, a very different kind of king from what they were expecting, the religious leaders in Jerusalem crucified Jesus, Acts 2:23 (***cross***).

◆ However, the Father raised Jesus from the dead (***open tomb***) and exalted Him (***glorified Jesus***), Acts 2:32–33. At Pentecost, God sent the Holy Spirit (***dove***) to empower people to understand and believe in Jesus the Messiah. The Holy Spirit adopts people into Jesus' Messianic community through Holy Baptism (***drop of water***), and empowers them for life in servant community through the Lord's Supper (***bread and cup***).

Lower section

These events paved the way for the fulfillment of what Jesus Himself had predicted, Luke 24:46,47. Acts tells us how, after Pentecost, witness to Jesus spread stage by stage from Jerusalem, the *capital of old Israel*, to Rome, the *capital of the Gentile world* (***concentric circles spreading out from Jerusalem to Rome, cross extending from Jerusalem to Rome***).

The exciting events outlined in Acts describe the spread of the Gospel:

> From ***Jerusalem***
>> to ***Samaria*** (Acts 8:1–40),
>> to Judea (8:26),
>> to ***Caesarea*** (8:40; 10:1–48),
>> to ***Damascus*** (9:1–9),
>> to Phoenicia, Cyprus (***Salamis***, ***Paphos***), ***Antioch*** (11:19),
>> to the Roman provinces of: Cilicia,
>>> Galatia (***Derbe***, ***Lystra***, ***Iconium***, ***Antioch*** (12:25–14:28),
>>> Asia (***Perga***, ***Attalia***, ***Ephesus***),
>>> Macedonia (***Philippi***, ***Thessalonica***, ***Beroea***),
>>> Achaia (***Athens***, ***Corinth***) (16:1–18:22; 18:23–21:17),
>>>> and finally to ***Rome*** (28:16).

God's people have witnessed to Jesus down through the ages, and will continue to do so until Jesus returns. Although outward conditions in the world have changed, God has not changed the witness His people are to give. **Jesus the Messiah is God's eternal, changeless Truth.**

In the world of the early Church, many found it difficult to discover God's real truth. Numerous persuasive teachers traveled around offering a variety of teachings. Although they were sincere, their sincerity did not validate what they taught. When the early apostles began working among Gentiles (non-Jews), they found themselves having to contend with numerous false teachings.

 A heresy which challenged and troubled the early Church (and which remains in various forms today) was Gnosticism. Gnosticism taught that God is all spirit. (*Although this illustration uses the same symbol for God, the Gnostic "god" was very different from the God revealed in the Bible.*) It taught that God has nothing to do with matter of any kind, and did not create the material world. However, the Gnostics claimed that God did create numerous lesser divine beings referred to as *aeons* or *emanations* (depicted in **ILLUSTRATION 30B** by *crowns* on which are **astrological symbols**). The most distant of these made the *material world* (**top half of Planet Earth complete with plant life**, *bottom center*) and the *human race* (**human figure standing on Planet Earth**).

 The Gnostics taught that fragments of *divine light* (**flame on symbol for God**) drifted away (***first arrow making up the yellow dashed circle***) from God's presence and took up residence in people on Planet Earth (***flame on human figure***). More, they became virtually imprisoned within human bodies.

 These *fragments of divine light* did not know how to escape, or that they should even try to escape. They did not know the way back to God (as the Gnostics understood God). They forgot where they came from. The Gnostics therefore saw the problem as *ignorance*, and the solution as gaining *knowledge* (hence *Gnostic*, from the Greek word for "knowledge")—depicted by a ***black lamp with a red flame***.

 When the divine element within the physical body gained sufficient knowledge about its origins and its present condition, it could escape from its captivity within the body and return to its place of origin. Involved in this process was the need for the divine element to learn the necessary passwords to enable it to get safely past any aeons or emanations it might encounter on the return journey to God. This notion is depicted by the fragment of divine light (***flame**, upper right*) on its way back (***second arrow making up the yellow dashed circle***) to the divine presence.

 In view of the fact that the human body is merely material matter, and one day will be thrown on this earthly dust heap, what are those *possessing enlightened spirits* to do with their physical bodies while waiting for that moment when the divine would escape from the physical? The Gnostics offered two answers:

    a.   Some suggested that a person could devote the human body to any use. After all, it was material and would be discarded at death. Therefore, why not indulge its appetites? "Eat, drink and be merry!" (*Antinomianism, lower left*)

    b.   Others taught that the enlightened should bring the body's appetites under control: "touch not, taste not, handle not." (*Legalism, lower right*. Gnostics were in bondage—***chains***—to ***law-codes***.)

When we understand Gnosticism, we become more aware of the challenge the early apostles faced as they sought to give witness about Jesus in various parts of the Mediterranean world.

30C

JESUS   'CHRIST'   'CHRIST'   JESUS
        COMES   DEPARTS   DIES

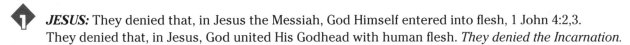

ILLUSTRATION 30C depicts the views of those who mixed together Gnosticism and Christianity.

1 *JESUS:* They denied that, in Jesus the Messiah, God Himself entered into flesh, 1 John 4:2,3. They denied that, in Jesus, God united His Godhead with human flesh. *They denied the Incarnation.*

2 *'CHRIST' COMES':* They taught that when Jesus was baptized (**drop of water**), the "Christ" or "divine element" (**halo**) took up residence in the man Jesus. The goal of the "Christ" was to bring knowledge and wisdom (**black lamp with red flame**) to the divine spirit held captive in human bodies.

3 *'CHRIST' DEPARTS:* After completing this mission, the "Christ" departed from the body of Jesus and returned to the spiritual realm of the divine (**rising halo**).

4 *JESUS DIES:* They said that only **the man Jesus** went to the cross, not the divine Son of God, Jesus the Messiah. *They denied Jesus' resurrection and the atonement.*

The "Christian" Gnostics insisted that people need *knowledge*, not *forgiveness*, and looked down on those lesser creatures incapable of taking in their superior knowledge. They did not treat sin seriously, and did not exhort people to love and serve one another, 1 John 1:8,9; 4:20,21.

The apostle John exhorts us, "Test the spirits to see whether they are from God," 1 John 4:1. False beliefs and practices continue to abound, but many are merely old heresies in new dress. The four elements of Gnostic belief outlined above serve as a useful touchstone to "test the spirits." Of teaching being offered as "Christian," we need to ask:

◆ Does it present Jesus the Messiah as God entered into flesh?

◆ Does it treat seriously the reality and consequences of human sin?

◆ Does it teach that Jesus the Messiah atoned for the sin of the world through His perfect life, vicarious death, and victorious resurrection?

◆ Does it exhort those "in Christ" to devote life to the loving service of God and others?

References to, and warnings against, Gnostic teachings are found in 1 and 2 Corinthians, Ephesians, Colossians, 1 and 2 Timothy, Titus, 2 Peter, 1 and 2 John, Jude and the Revelation to John.

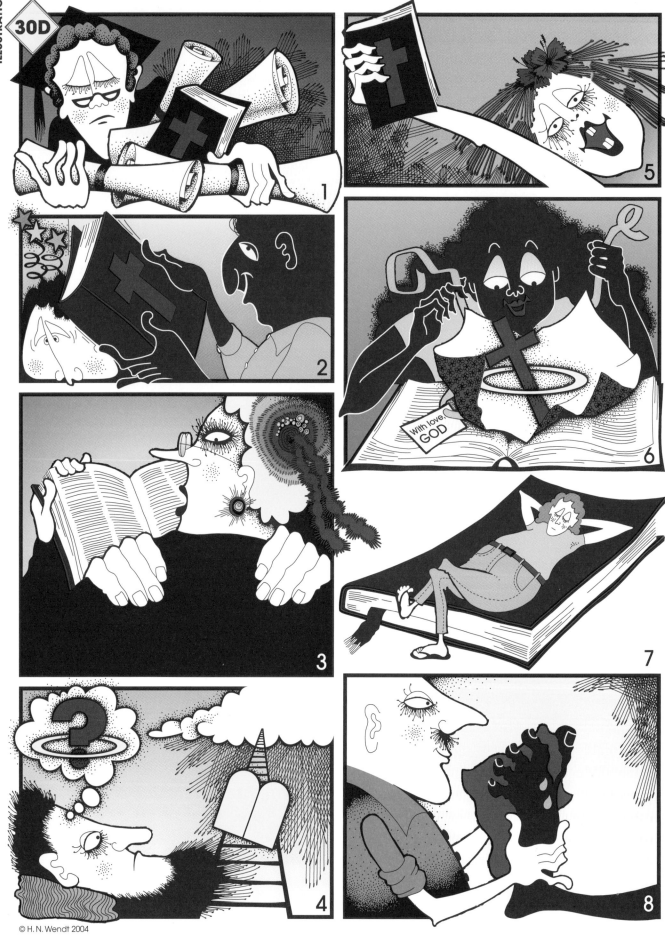

...in your heart and life since you began working through the central truths of the Bible using these materials?

ILLUSTRATION 30D portrays some of the thoughts that go through people's minds as they contemplate doing Bible study, or as they actually do it. (The numbers below correspond to those in the illustration.)

1 Some do it merely to collect a **diploma** or a **certificate**, or perhaps to please someone else.

2 Some undertake Bible study to equip themselves to win arguments about religion. They plan to use the Bible to bash others (*note the **victim** in the lower left corner*).

3 Many people are afraid to take a Bible into *their* **hands**. They fear that it might get *its* hands on them! They are partly right—for indeed, through the Bible, God seeks to draw people to Himself in "the embrace of grace" (**hands on woman's shoulders**).

4 Some have the mistaken notion that the Bible contains nothing but commandments they must try to keep if they are to make it to and through the "pearly gates" into heaven, into God's presence (**cloud**). Often they are not sure (**question mark**) they want to be all that good (**halo**).

5 When we spend time reading the Bible, we find that it offers us a message that is all joy and good news (**happy face**)!

6 The Bible offers each of us personally a grand gift—the forgiveness of sins through Jesus' **cross**, and membership in God's community of saints (**halo**).

7 When God brings us to faith in Jesus the Messiah, God does not call us to **rest on His Word** (*as on a mattress*), but instead to that true rest which is life in fellowship with Jesus, Matthew 11:28–30. The person depicted is confusing Christian *vocation* with Christian *vacation*.

8 Jesus calls His followers to serve one another—even as Jesus served His disciples, John 13:1–15 (**person washing another person's feet**).

The journey through the biblical narrative is a long and challenging one. Those who have made that journey, using **THE DIVINE DRAMA** as their road-map, will be familiar with the symbols used in **ILLUSTRATION 30E** and the message of those symbols.

The following paragraph, written by H.G. Wells, summarizes the challenge that Jesus the Messiah posed and continues to pose for humanity (*Outline of History*, Vol. 1, pp. 425–61).

> *Jesus was too great for His disciples. And in view of what He plainly said, is it any wonder that all who were rich and prosperous felt a horror of strange things, a swimming of their world at His teaching? Perhaps the priests and rulers and rich men understood Him better than His followers. He was dragging out all the little private reservations they had made from social service into the light of a universal religious life. He was like a terrible moral huntsman, digging mankind out of the snug burrows in which they had lived hitherto. In the white blaze of His kingdom there was to be no property, no privilege, no pride and no precedence, no motive and reward but love. Is it any wonder that men were dazzled and blinded, and cried out against Him? Even His disciples cried out when He would not spare them that light. Is it any wonder that the priests realized that between this man and themselves there was no choice, but that He or their priestcraft should perish? Is it any wonder that the Roman soldiers, confronted and amazed by something soaring over their comprehension and threatening all their disciplines, should take refuge in wild laughter, and crown Him with thorns, and robe Him in purple, and make a mock Caesar of Him? For to take Him seriously was to enter into a strange and alarming life, to abandon habits, to control instincts and impulses, and to embrace an incredible happiness. Is it any wonder that to this day this Galilean is too much for our small hearts?*

May the Holy Spirit inspire and empower us to *believe*, *reflect*, and *share* the message of ILLUSTRATION 30E. Indeed, may the Holy Spirit empower us to give the Galilean, Jesus the Messiah, plenty of space in our small hearts!

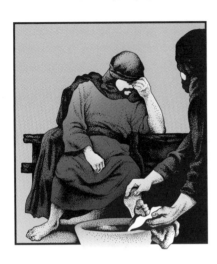

30A During the Pentecost observance described in Acts 2, the Holy Spirit empowered the disciples to witness to Jesus, crucified and risen, as the promised Messianic King and as the Lord of time and eternity. The Book of Acts outlines how witness to Jesus spread out from Jerusalem across the Mediterranean world until it reached Rome, the capital of the Gentile world.

30B When the apostles began witnessing to Jesus in the Gentile world, they had to deal with a heresy known as Gnosticism. The Gnostics denied that God made the material universe or the human body. According to the Gnostics, the real world was the invisible world of spirit. They taught that the goal of life was to acquire knowledge so that they might eventually escape the material world and partake of the world of spirit. What were people to do with their material body while waiting for that final deliverance? Some said, "*Indulge* its appetites." Others said, "*Restrain* its appetites."

30C The Gnostics denied the reality of sin, Jesus' incarnation, atoning work, resurrection, and ascension. Furthermore, they issued no call to live a life of loving service to others. For them, the goal of life was to acquire knowledge!

30D People undertake a study of the Bible for a variety of reasons— some good, some not so good. Even so, God can use any contact people have with His Word to bring people to a knowledge of their sin, and their need of Jesus' saving ministry. The Bible's message is an invitation to a joyous, meaningful life. It reveals to us God's gift of the forgiveness of sins through Jesus the Messiah, and calls us to use life to glorify God by serving others.

30E **The good and gracious will of God is that God's people embrace in faith, and follow in servanthood, Jesus the Messiah, so that they might live already in this life as they will in the life to come.**